Jubilee Time

Also by Maria Harris

Dance of the Spirit

The D.R.E. Book

The D.R.E. Reader

Experiences in Community
(with Gabriel Moran)

The Faith of Parents

Fashion Me a People

Parish Religious Education

Teaching and Religious Imagination

Women and Teaching

Jubilee Time

Celebrating Women, Spirit, and the Advent of Age

Maria Harris

BANTAM BOOKS

New York   Toronto   London   Sydney   Auckland

A Bantam Book / August 1995

The author expresses gratitude to the following for granting permission to quote from their work:
Jenny Joseph's "Warning," from *Selected Poems*, published by Bloodaxe Books, Newcastle-upon-Tyne.
Copyright © Jenny Joseph 1992; to Princeton University Press to quote from James B. Pritchard,
Ancient Near Eastern Texts Relating to the Old Testament © 1955; to Random House for lines from Muriel
Rukeyser's "Kathe Kollwitz," III, in *The Speed of Darkness* (New York: Random House, 1968); from
"Unlearning to Not Speak" by Marge Piercy, which appears in *Circles on the Water*, Alfred A. Knopf,
1982. Copyright © 1971, 1982 by Marge Piercy and Middlemarsh, Inc. Used by permission of the
Wallace Literary Agency, Inc.; Scripture quotations from the New Revised Standard Version of the
Bible, © 1989 by the Division of Christian Education of the National Council of the Churches of
Christ in the USA, all rights reserved. The first lines of Psalms 118 and 138 are from *Psalms Anew*,
translated by Maureen Leach and Nancy Schreck. Used by permission of St. Mary's Press, Winona,
MN; from *For Colored Girls Who Have Considered Suicide / When the Rainbow Is Enuf* by Ntozake Shange.
Reprinted with permission of Simon and Schuster. Copyright © 1975, 1976, 1977 by Ntozake Shange;
from "Dirge Without Music" by Edna St. Vincent Millay. From *Collected Poems*, HarperCollins.
Copyright © 1928, 1955 by Edna St. Vincent Millay and Norma Millay Ellis. Reprinted by
permission of Elizabeth Barnett, literary executor.

BOOK DESIGN BY DONNA SINISGALLI

Library of Congress Cataloging-in-Publication Data
Harris, Maria.
Jubilee time : celebrating women, spirit, and the
advent of age / Maria Harris.
p.   cm.
Includes bibliographical references and index.
ISBN 0-553-09986-8
1. Middle aged women—Religious life.
2. Spiritual life—Christianity.   3. Spiritual
exercises.   I. Title.
BV4579.5.H38   1995
248.8′43—dc20   94-45164
                                                                        CIP
Published simultaneously in the United States and Canada

Bantam Books are published by Bantam Books, a division of Bantam Doubleday Dell Publishing
Group, Inc. Its trademark, consisting of the words "Bantam Books" and the portrayal of a rooster, is
Registered in U.S. Patent and Trademark Office and in other countries. Marca Registrada.
Bantam Books, 1540 Broadway, New York, New York 10036.

PRINTED IN THE UNITED STATES OF AMERICA
FFG   10   9   8   7   6   5   4   3   2   1

For Joan Grace
and for my coauthors,
with gratitude and affection

You shall hallow the fiftieth year; and you shall proclaim liberty throughout the land to all its inhabitants. For it is a jubilee; it shall be holy to you.

—The Book of Leviticus

CONTENTS

$\mathcal{A}$CKNOWLEDGMENTS

No one writes a book alone; I am no exception. But *Jubilee Time* is coauthored in a special way. Not only does it draw on the ideas and thoughts of those who work with or have written on women, aging, spirituality, and their interconnections, it includes the reflections of over 135 women who graciously responded to a questionnaire I sent out on these issues, and the shared ideas of many others willing to have conversations with me on the topic. Almost all, when asked, said, "Of course, use my name, and use my responses," and the reader will find this a richer book because of that. I have tried to express my gratitude personally to each of these women; here I do it publicly, with deep appreciation. In addition, I offer special thanks to those women who not only responded themselves, but sent the questionnaire along to friends and acquaintances—I will say more about them in the Introduction.

I also wish to acknowledge the wisdom of the Jewish thinkers who have shaped my understandings of several of the themes in this book, especially Sabbath and Gratitude. As one raised outside of Judaism, I have nonetheless found the work of Sherry Blumberg, Abraham Joshua Heschel, Sara Lee, Jo

Milgrom, Judith Plaskow, Letty Cottin Pogrebin and Lilly Rivlin, among others, invaluable. But in a special way, as a Christian, I am also indebted to the rich, poetic, ever-fruitful Jewish tradition itself, not only past but present. I am nourished continually by its insights, and as a "stranger in its land," to use a Jubilee phrase, I acknowledge my indebtedness to the people of that land.

I'm also grateful to those who've invited me to spend several days or a week with groups of women—and at times men too—who wanted to pursue the themes of Jubilee, and to those who took part in those groups, sharing their lives with me as they did. These include Lyn Yeo, Lowell Moyse, Marion Moyse, and close to one hundred participants in Kingston, Ontario; retreatants and "regulars" at Cor Maria, a Sag Harbor, New York, retreat house; the Jubilee women convened by Rita Clare Dorner at Santa Clara University; an articulate and reflective group gathered in Holland, Michigan, by George Brown, especially Linda Lee Albert, Sheila Frank, and Noel Horn; the wise and witty women of Bethsaida, led by Jeanne McGorry; Barb Nardi and the women I met at Cathedral House in Corpus Christi; Pat Duffy and the sabbatical groups in Water Mill, Long Island; the religious educators of Phoenix, Arizona, especially John and Mary Ann Meyer; Judi Geake and the Women's Exchange members in Winnetka, Illinois; seminar attendees in Princeton, New Jersey, who alerted me to the power of "every seventh year" so crucial to Jubilee; Pat Luparello and Grace Harding of Pittsburgh; Rita Brill and Jackie Foster of Boise, Idaho; Maria Kleinschmidt of Little Rock; Sue Bertoletti of Lansdale, Pennsylvania; Kathy Gadjos and the women at Temenos Spiritual Center in Broad Run, Pennsylvania; and not least, Sheila Carney, RSM, president of the Pittsburgh Sisters of Mercy, who has continually affirmed and supported the power of Jubilee in the spirituality of women as we age. I must also thank Joyce Cupps, editor and founder of *Encore: The Return of the Crone,* who initiated my regular Jubilee column in that fine magazine for older women, and Michelle Rapkin and Maria Mack, who shepherded my original proposal for *Jubilee Time* to acceptance by Bantam.

Several other institutional opportunities enabled me to develop the material in the book: invitations to teach at Auburn Theological Seminary in New York and to deliver several lectures, including the Education Lectures at Candler School of Theology in Atlanta; the Alumnae/Alumni Lectures at Columbia Seminary in Decatur, Georgia; the Schaff Lectures at Pittsburgh Theological Seminary; the McFadin Lectures at Brite Divinity School in Fort Worth; and the Bradner Lectures at Virginia Theological Seminary in Arlington. The feedback and the conversations and contact with those who came to listen and to speak with me in those settings taught me a great deal.

Finally, coming closer to the center of my personal Jubilee Time, I must attempt to express my gratitude to five other people. To my extraordinarily gifted editor at Bantam, Linda Gross, I offer what can be only a feeble thank-you, in the light of your thoughtful counsel and artistic sensitivity in pushing me toward excellence with each succeeding draft of *Jubilee Time.*

To Kathy Sperduto and Joanmarie Smith I offer this simple acknowledgment: without you, I couldn't have done it—your careful criticism, love, and listening mean the world to me.

To Gabriel Moran, the partner with whom I am blessed to be growing old, my daily prayer of wonder for the gift of your presence.

And to Joan Grace, one of the coauthors to whom I dedicate this book, I express the honor it is to be your friend. Stranger to neither laughter nor loss, you are a Jubilee woman par excellence and a grace to everyone you touch.

Maria Harris
Montauk, New York
August 1994

$\mathcal{I}$NTRODUCTION

*You shall count off seven weeks of years, seven times seven years, so that
the time of the seven weeks of years shall be to you forty-nine years.
Then you shall hallow the fiftieth year. It shall be a jubilee for you.*

Lev. 25:8, 10

With these words as summons, I invite you to enter Jubilee
Time. I ask you to join me in exploring the biblical Jubilee, a
feast celebrating the fiftieth year and providing the basis of a
spirituality for women in the second half of life. Too little
known, the many facets of Jubilee are gifts to every woman
facing who she is now and what she might become in the
years and decades following her fiftieth birthday.

The first mention of Jubilee occurs in the Hebrew Bible,
in the twenty-fifth chapter of the Book of Leviticus. There, a
caring, attentive God speaks to a weary, exhausted people who
are entering a new chapter in their lives. "When you enter the
land I am giving you," says this God, "the land shall observe a
Sabbath. Six years you shall sow your field, and six years you

shall prune your vineyards and gather in their yield; but in the seventh year there shall be a Sabbath of complete rest for the land, a Sabbath for the Lord."

This people's God begins by establishing a foundation of rest and re-creation—a spirituality—for them. From the beginning of their sojourn in the new land, they are to alternate work and withdrawal from work. This creates a rhythmic pattern that increases in momentum with every seven-year cycle. During those sabbatical years, they are to step back from their ordinary routines and practice a reverent attitude toward one another, the land, and themselves. They are to forgive debts and return property. They are to honor the Divine Mystery Who is their origin. As they do they become readied for the great ritual of Jubilee.

Finally it arrives:

You shall count off seven weeks of years, seven times seven years, so that the period of seven weeks of years gives forty-nine years. Then you shall have the trumpet sounded loud; on the tenth day of the seventh month—on the day of atonement—you shall have the trumpet sounded throughout all your land.

And you shall hallow the fiftieth year, and you shall proclaim liberty throughout the land to all its inhabitants; it shall be a jubilee for you; you shall return, every one of you, to your property and every one of you to your family.

That fiftieth year shall be a jubilee for you; you shall not sow, or reap the aftergrowth, or harvest the unpruned vines. For it is a jubilee; it shall be holy to you. (Lev. 25:8–12)

Ceasing work the way Jubilee commands—no sowing, reaping, or harvesting—is not a counsel to idleness. Instead, it is an opportunity to begin a process and to fashion an approach to life that embodies a very specific spirituality. This spirituality emerges from the command to hallow the fiftieth year. For once the fiftieth year arrives, work differing from that of earlier decades takes precedence. The work involves crossing boundaries, pausing to hallow our lives and our land, and proclaiming liberty to all the earth's inhabitants. It involves revisiting and honoring ancestors, making mature assessments and judgments, and giving shape to individual stories. Each of these eventually spills over into a great song of praise and gratitude that affirms and completes life, even in the face of inevitable death.

In *Jubilee Time,* I offer each of these works as a component of spirituality for women in life's second half. Although the biblical Jubilee is just as appropriate for men as for women, I have found that a variety of social, spiritual, historical, and biological factors mark the years after fifty as an especially fruitful time in the lives of women, and that our particular era is ripe with conditions that foster this fruitfulness.

I also offer each of these works as a *ritual,* a consciously shaped process and way of acting that includes specific steps. Rituals help particular groups of people to interpret themselves at important times in their lives: people in the United States celebrate the memory of their country's birth on the Fourth of July; the Jones family gathers for Susan and Samuel's wedding; the senior class graduates from high school as a rite of passage into adult life. But rituals also carry a spiritual power, especially when associated with the inner life. They point beyond what ordinary speech and action can convey.

Drawing on Jubilee, the rituals in this book are designed to help women interpret the second half of their lives. The first ritual is Crossing the Threshold, based on the biblical experience of entering a new land, and designed for women making the rite of passage into the land of age. This is followed by the Hallowing of Sabbath, a response to the command to "keep a Sabbath of complete rest," and to the older woman's discovery that as she takes possession of her life she needs on occasion to say no. Then comes the ritual of Proclaiming Freedom, which observes the Jubilee counsel to "proclaim liberty throughout the land to all its inhabitants," and to work for justice toward everyone, including our older selves. This leads into the Jubilee Journeys, the ritual returns to place and people, family and heritage—as important to women of age as it was to the first Jubilarians.

Having made the return to place and people, the next two rituals enable us to return to ourselves. One, based on Jubilee's commands to "count off" and examine our relations to possessions, power, and persons, helps us take an Inventory of our lives. Having done that, the Jubilee woman can then accomplish the return to herself made possible by memory. Imitating the first Jubilee people, whose story begins with the counsel, "Remember: I your God led you out of the land of Egypt and into the land of Canaan," we engage in the ritual act of Telling Our Story, including the naming of our own Egypts and our own Canaans.

These rituals culminate in a final step, based on the opening verses of Jubilee but equally fitting at its conclusion: "You shall have the trumpet sounded loud; you shall have the trumpet sounded loud throughout all your land. For it is a jubilee: it shall be holy to you." The time has come for celebration, festivity, and thanksgiving. The time has come to render thanks for a life, for a calling, for a Giver at the heart of it all. The time has come to sing the Song of Gratitude.

The Hebrew word *yobel,* translated as "trumpet," is the word for a ram's horn sounded in times of celebration and rejoicing. Besides the Jubilee citation in the Book of Leviticus, the sixth chapter of Joshua mentions the *yobel,* when the trumpet sounds and the walls of Jericho come tumbling down. *Yobel* is one of the words from which we get the more familiar *jubilee.* The other is the verb *ybl,* which means a royal release from bondage and a return or a bringing back.

Both derivations give important insights into Jubilee Time. Each of Jubilee's rituals has an essential connection to release, return, and forgiveness, especially toward those undergoing crushing debt or loss of land. Each of the rituals is also cause for celebration. As the basis of a spirituality for women living in Jubilee Time, each acts as a touchstone and a promise. For like those ancient Israelites, we too are entering a period of royal release, freed to become all that we are meant to be, committed to bringing the walls of ageism tumbling down at last. For those of us who are or are about to become Jubilee women, the trumpet is sounding.

ONE WOMAN'S JOURNEY INTO JUBILEE

My personal path to the Book of Leviticus and into the rituals of Jubilee Time began in 1980 when, at the age of 48, I had my first sabbatical. I'd been a teacher and educational administrator since 1952, but had never held a position where a sabbatical—a paid leave from work, enabling rest and re-creation—was part of the job. But in 1980, I was teaching outside Boston at Andover Newton Theological School, a graduate school of theology that prepared people for religious professions such as parish ministry, hospital chaplaincy, spiritual direction, and pastoral care. At the school, after nine and a half semesters "on," professors were granted one semester "off." I'd lucked out by teaching at a place combining the two modern professions that still grant regular sabbaticals: academic life and ministry.

I had a lovely five months. My professional interest at the time was the intersection of religion and education, especially the teaching of spirituality, so I journeyed to England to study contemporary accounts of religious experience being researched at Oxford University's Manchester College. There I had time to study on my own terms, at my own pace. I also had time to do nothing. I could be still, read, hold unhurried conversations, break for a cup of tea, sleep through breakfast—the choice was mine.

One of my readings during this period was a brief essay by my colleague Meg Funk. During a period when she'd been briefly ill, Meg wrote, she'd been forced to rest and stop work. Slowed down, and casting about for reading, she'd discovered Rabbi Abraham Joshua Heschel's spiritual classic, *The Sabbath.* She described how reading it led her to ask about Sabbath in her own life and in the lives of all the busy people she knew. She described Sabbath as a divine commandment, one of the Ten, but pointed out that in our world, many of us don't have time for it. We're too busy running and producing to engage in a practice that can slow us down and inevitably change our lives.

Her words touched me so deeply that I immediately sought out Heschel's book and read it avidly. It spoke of Sabbath as a sacred dwelling, a palace in time that was not a date but an atmosphere. It shed light on the search I was making into the meanings of spirituality and on my personal longings for stillness, wholeness, and connection. At that time, however, I did not consciously relate Rabbi Heschel's book to either my sabbatical or my age.

When I returned to the States, I resumed my work as teacher and mentor in the realm of spirituality. In particular, I continued my exploration of women's spirituality, which eventually led to the publication of *Women and Teaching* and *Dance of the Spirit.*

I also continued my study of Sabbath and found it had multiple meanings. Not only was there a seventh-day and a seventh-year Sabbath; there was the forty-eight-hour Sabbath of Pentecost and the seventy-year Sabbath that represented the exile of the Jews in Babylon and, by implication, an entire human life.

Finally, there was the Sabbath of the Jubilee—a two-year period from the forty-ninth through the fiftieth year known as the "Sabbath of Sabbaths."

I remember the gradual, profoundly personal character of my Jubilee realization, taking me well beyond my initial intellectual curiosity. The first light came from Dennis, a former student. "When did you first become interested in Sabbath?" he asked, and I responded it was during my time in England. "But of course that fits," he responded. "After all, you were on sabbatical."

And when was that sabbatical? It had come at the dawning of my forty-ninth year, as I was counting up seven years of seven years.

On a winter evening in Lexington, Massachusetts, the last piece fell into place. After lecturing on Sabbath spirituality, I noticed an intense and interesting audience reaction during the discussion period. Rather than pick up on and pursue the seventh-day Sabbath, the Pentecost Sabbath of forty-eight hours, or the seventy-year Sabbath—each of which I'd mentioned—my listeners wanted to focus on the Sabbath of the Jubilee. When we dispersed, my good friend Charity Rowley came up to talk with me. "Why the interest in the Jubilee?" I asked her. "What was that about?"

She needed no time to think, answering immediately, "Maria, I can't speak for the others here, but I can tell you about me. I'm about to have my fiftieth birthday. Even the few words you offered about the Jubilee Sabbath tonight led me to think about a spirituality for the time that's approaching in my life; a spirituality that begins by hallowing the fiftieth year."

Her words struck home. By then I was in my early fifties. Her comments, linked with those of Dennis the previous summer, illuminated with a brilliant and steady light what was happening in my own life: my ache for stillness and quiet; my journeys; my interest in spirituality as it affected women's lives; my yearnings to return to my place and my people (I moved from Boston back to New York soon after my conversation with Charity and married the man I'd loved for years)—all were symbols I was living the Jubilee.

The music of my particular Jubilee trumpet was clear, and its rhythm carried me naturally into this book. I became pregnant with *Jubilee Time.*

The first steps toward writing it were my own reading and research. Besides biblical commentaries on the text of Leviticus 25, the work of two authors was invaluable to me—although neither is responsible for any conclusions I draw in this book. One is Sharon Ringe, who has written on the relation between the biblical Jubilee, liberation, and Jesus of Nazareth. The other is John Howard Yoder, who has written on the implications of the Jubilee for modern times.

I also sought out writing by women elders who reflect directly on aging women, and found some wonderful memoirs, most of which I quote from later in the book. Notable among these women are May Sarton, M.F.K. Fisher, Baba Copper, Doris Grumbach, and Florida Scott-Maxwell. I'd read Sarton and Scott-Maxwell before, but this time they spoke to me spirit to spirit so that my reaction was, "Of course. I *know* what you mean."

Simultaneously, I began participating in and leading workshops on older women's lives. One marvelous afternoon in New York's Soho, for example, I attended a workshop celebrating older birthdays at The Crystal Quilt, a women's center. That day Mina Hamilton led a circle of eighteen women through a powerful opening exercise I have subsequently used in my own teaching. Mina asked us to introduce ourselves as we moved around the circle, telling one another not only our names but our ages. To my amazement, no one minded. Instead, from Betty in her late seventies to the 33-year-old reporter who was covering the session for *New York Newsday,* every woman present proudly spoke her years: "I'm 67," "I'm 54," "I'm 70," "I'm 48." We were in a circle where it was safe to be the ages we were.

The final step toward writing *Jubilee Time* entailed sending out a brief questionnaire (see the Appendix) to a number of women with whom I didn't and couldn't have first-hand contact. At the same time I asked participants in workshops or retreats I was leading to take the time to fill it in. I wanted to verify my own ideas by checking out how other ordinary women were encountering the Jubilee years. I was also eager to find out how women who, unlike myself, were neither white nor, in some cases, living in the United States experienced the second half of life.

In this I had splendid help. Barbara Warren McCall shared my questionnaire at Pilgrim Place, a retirement center in Claremont, California. Kwok Pui-lan, a Chinese woman from Hong Kong with whom I was team-teaching, put me in touch with Asian-American women in the United States. My friend and former student Esther Byu, who chairs the Commission on Women for the Christian Conference of Asia, gathered responses from women on her side of the world that included Burmese, Malaysians, and New Zealanders (both Maori and Pakeha).

Here in the United States, Pastor Barbara Austin-Lucas asked African-American women in her congregation to respond, as did Regina Coll and Cathy Abeyta. In addition, Cathy sent the questionnaire to Hispanic and Latina women in several southwest states, and to Native American women of several tribes. Benedictine sister Mary Jo Torborg worked on my account with a group of elder Benedictine nuns in Minnesota; Marymount sister Ann Marino provided me entree to the women at Cor Maria I've already mentioned; Sarah Epperly introduced me to a group of older women writers from Connecticut. The women ranged in age from their mid-forties to ninety-three.

It was 56-year-old Sarah who gave me a special burst of confidence that my work was important and necessary. She not only filled out the questionnaire, but wrote back:

> I am so glad you are pursuing this inquiry. It is so important. Most of us women are living longer and

enjoying good health. We are anxious to be making our contribution and to be taken seriously as we do so. Yet I feel that I don't have many models to which I may refer. It seems to me that I am designing my life as I go along without any clear notion where I am going.

Affirmations such as that have kept me inspired in the work of creating *Jubilee Time* over the last five years. Almost all of the women who've spoken with me or written briefly about their coming of age have allowed me to cite them in the text. Although I want to be clear that the questionnaires and the respondents do not constitute a scientifically controlled survey, I am nevertheless convinced from their responses that the time for this book is now and the hunger for the kind of spirituality it fosters is real. They support me in the belief that something occurs in the late forties propelling us into new ways of living, new understandings of ourselves as women, new life tasks. They also convince me that *the* spirituality to guide us during this time is the biblical Jubilee, with its rituals of Crossing the Threshold, Hallowing the Sabbath, Proclaiming Freedom, The Jubilee Journeys, Taking Inventory, Telling Our Story, and Singing Our Gratitude.

INTO THE RITUALS

In turning now to each of these rituals, I encourage you, the reader, to take your time, to go slowly, and to savor the steps comprising each ritual. Some of you will be neophytes to Jubilee, still gathering up the seven-year periods as you move toward 49 and 50. Others of you will be veterans, "fierce with the reality of age" that Florida Scott-Maxwell describes. Most of you will be somewhere in between, as were the majority of women who responded to me.

Still, whatever your age, I believe the work you will be doing in Jubilee Time is holy work that demands your involvement. So as you take it on, grant yourself permission to give it all the time it needs. If you're able and it's not a crazy dream, take two years off. Keep a journal of your responses to the exercises in each chapter as a way of recording your interaction with each ritual; I've indicated in the text those places where pausing to do this seems to fit. Or, if you choose, read the book all the way through first and then go back and do the exercises that speak most compellingly to you. Gather with like-minded women, like those at The Crystal Quilt, so that you may find out how you are like other Jubilee women and how you differ. Trust your own spirit, your own pilgrimage, your own history. Trust yourself.

For if you do, re-creation and transformation can happen to you. Your re-creation, your transformation, will be as unique as your fingerprints, and no woman's Jubilee Time will be an exact replica of any other. Nevertheless, as you undertake the spirituality of Jubilee, most of you will be likely to find several things happening.

You will discover yourself embracing your inner elder with affection and wisdom, even as you may have already embraced your inner child.

You will observe yourself changing your own and society's understanding of the phrases "older woman" and "old woman" from something feared or degraded to something celebrated and revered.

You will experience yourself becoming a model and mentor for younger women who may be hesitant or reluctant to encounter their own aging.

And you will take on the role of midwife, bringing into existence a newborn woman eager to live the present, incorporate the past, and face the future. You will find yourself assisting at your own rebirth, not because you are reading about the discoveries I have made in my Jubilee years, but because you have encountered the richness and beauty of your own.

Jubilee Time

One

CROSSING THE THRESHOLD

Enter the land that I am giving you. . . .

Lev. 25:2

In the beginning is the threshold—the boundary, the point of departure. The opening lines of the biblical teaching on Jubilee describe God speaking to Moses on Mount Sinai, asking him to tell the people they will soon pass over into a new land. That land is a specific, identifiable area along the river Jordan, close to the Mediterranean Sea. Its name is Canaan. For the Israelites, the future of their people hinges on their entering it now. They must cross its threshold.

For women entering the second half of life, the beginning is also a threshold, and Jubilee Time starts with a summons to a region that is also specific and identifiable. This region differs from Canaan, however, because it is not a physical dwelling place, but a spiritual arena emerging from the midst of life as we enter our fiftieth year. Its name is Jubilee.

Jubilee is a place of maturity and wisdom, liberation and loss. Sometimes the summons to cross its threshold comes from an interior voice light as a whisper; sometimes through an incident loud as a trumpet. No matter the form of the summons, the message is the same. The first half of life is over, and something new aches, even demands, to be born. With the command to count up seven weeks of years and to hallow the fiftieth year, the Divine Mystery at the core of the universe beckons us into Jubilee Time. "Enter the land that I am giving you," sings the Holy One at creation's center, just as She did to the first Jubilee people. Now. Today. If you hear this summons, harden not your heart.

The call to cross a boundary is a recurring biblical theme from Genesis to Revelation. From the banishing of Adam and Eve from the mythical Eden, to the passage out of Egypt and on through the parting of the Sea of Reeds, to the final invitation to enter a New Jerusalem where death and mourning shall be no more, it resounds repeatedly. The Bible chronicles the saga of a people responding to that call, continually crossing thresholds as they dream of a land of milk and honey, enduring deserts and prisons and warfare as they search for an ultimate home.

That same call, with all its immediacy, risk, and excitement, breaks into the lives of Jubilee women today. We are being lured by the Creator Spirit, by our own inner spirit, and by life itself to a new perception of age and aging. We are being lured toward a spirituality that reflects who we are at this time of life, one that we create out of our own experiences and desires. We are being lured to open the doors of our hearts and the gates of our spirits. We are being lured across the threshold of Jubilee Time. Crossing it is our first ritual.

CROSSING THRESHOLDS

Crossing a threshold is a sacred, ritual act, not only in the Bible, but throughout human history. Thresholds have always been granted special powers. In most cultures, pride of place goes to the door and the doorway, especially in the home. In ancient Rome, Janus was the god of the house door, safeguarding entry. In Babylonia, Egypt, and Israel, judgments were made and handed down at the threshold. In Palestine, a mother couldn't nurse or scold her child on the threshold; according to one folk belief, punishing a child there could make it seriously ill. In the nineteenth century, the front-door entrance in Britain was christened the "fresh wood." And although the custom seems to be dying out, many of us were carried over a threshold as young brides, symbolizing the movement into marriage, away from the homes of our youth.

In time the threshold took on its fullest spiritual significance as entry into the sacred space and hallowed time where communication with divinity and the gods is possible. A threshold is a place of the spirit, uniting the mundane with the mysterious and the commonplace with the awesome. Entering Jubilee, we cross this kind of threshold. Ready to take possession of our entire lives, both our youth and our maturity, we move into a new spiritual landscape. With the Psalmist we find ourselves poised to sing the ancient entrance hymn and make its closing verses our own:

Breathing the Threshold

To help you enter this ritual and claim the threshold of your own Jubilee Time, this exercise directs you to center on the word *threshold*.

Begin by sitting comfortably—in a quiet place if possible, but on a bus or a train if necessary. If you are at home, light a candle as a symbol of the sacredness of these moments.

    When you are ready, close your eyes, and pay attention to your breathing, first inhaling as you slowly count, "One, two, three, four," and then exhaling on "One, two, three, four." Do this several times—for five or ten breaths—until you feel yourself growing calm.

Fling wide the gates,
    open the ancient doors,
    and the Holy One will come in!

(PSALM 24)

A NEW ORIENTATION

The fiftieth year is the orientation point for the threshold of Jubilee Time, although we discover that subsequent birthdays—55, 65, 70, 75, 80, 90—serve as reorientations as we grow older. The word *orientation* actually has a spiritual origin;

When you have become calm, allow the word *threshold* to surface in your consciousness. Repeat the word *threshold* as you inhale and exhale, once again for five or ten breaths. When you have done this, gently explore the following questions:

1. Who—or what—is the Holy One waiting to enter your life?
2. What threshold does the Holy One bid you to cross?
3. What obstacles, if any, hold you back?
4. What energies draw you forth?
5. What are the first steps you must take to cross this threshold?

After gentle and unhurried meditation on these questions, complete the exercise by a repetition of the word *threshold*.

Return to this exercise at least twice more during the day, perhaps before you cross the threshold into sleep.

it comes from the custom of building churches along an east-west axis. The altar end of a church points toward the morning or "orient," where the sun rises.

The sun orients Jubilee women too. But now it's nearer the western horizon, creating the resplendent colors accompanying sunset as well as the lengthening shadows prefiguring age and death. Our orientation is toward the setting sun and toward completing the cycle that makes life whole. Perhaps for the first time in history we've ceased denying this and instead are learning to turn confidently in its direction.

Barbara, a 77-year-old magazine editor who climbed the Himalayas in her sixties, and who has been a friend for several decades, captured this meaning of the orient in a singularly poetic reflection. "What's an image you'd use to describe this time of life?" I asked her. She thought carefully and finally answered, "I see the sun sinking toward the horizon. The colors of the sunset are gorgeous. There's a road approaching the sunset and I'm walking along the road, stopping to look at things beside the path, and finding each more beautiful than the one before." She's not only accepting but celebrating the orientation of Jubilee Time as the direction her life is taking.

As a facet of a mature spirituality, that acceptance begins in our late forties and early fifties, when we first confront the reality of Jubilee. The departure of children from home, the reduction of job demands, and the changes in our bodies make us aware we're facing a new social and biological orientation. But that prompts the discovery that we're also facing a new *spiritual* orientation and being offered the opportunity to enter a state of grace where we slow down, find our contemplative center, and create a new way of being in the world that suits us in the land of age.

Although my hunch was that real older women (as distinct from stock characters or media stereotypes) didn't fear age, I was still delightfully surprised when, talking with me about the threshold of aging, women expressed a nearly universal excitement. When they arrived at the portal described in the Bible as the "land God is giving us," they decided to open it. When they did, they found the sympathetic and appealing mercies of Jubilee awaiting them.

Many reported experiencing themselves on the verge of something pristine, whether they were new to Jubilee Time or decades into it. This was true of Anita, who at 51 wrote, "I'm just beginning to know who I am. I'm just venturing out to see things and learn how to live." It was true of Paula too, who wrote, "At 72, I feel great about growing old. Once I accepted some of the natural aging limitations, life took on new challenges and new interest." Melanie, 67, rejoiced: "I still feel green and full of sap." And 53-year-old Beverly declared, "I feel excited. It's as if I'm about to set out on a very special vacation—one I've been waiting for for many years. I've been planning and now the time is here." (See Exercise 1.)

EASING THE PASSAGE

Not all rituals can lay claim to being what anthropologists call "rites of passage," those whose central dynamic marks change and transition. But as the Jubilee ritual most concerned with traversing previously uncrossed borders, this threshold ritual asserts itself as precisely such a rite.

Many societies celebrate the passage into maturity. The Chinese practice a tradition where visitors greet their hosts with the question, "And what is your glorious age?" If the host responds, "Thirty" or "Forty," the visitor gives a sad shake of the head or offers a gesture of sympathy. But if the person questioned names a greater age, the visitor's face brightens with delight, shining with increasing intensity the higher the age reported.

In contrast and until recently, Western society denigrated this passage. Seventy-one-year-old Mary is not alone in naming the worst thing about growing old as "ageism—leading people to fear aging so much they literally make older people like me feel invisible." Although new, more positive understandings of terms such as *crone* and *witch* are now circulating, more negative terms, especially for aging women, continue to pervade our language. "Old Master" is a positive term of regard, but "Old Mistress"? "Old maid"? "Little old lady in tennis shoes"?

Recent active resistance to such language and the attitudes underlying it are helping to ease the passage into later life. The aging of the baby boomers; the public visibility of more and more older women, such as Toni Morrison, Sandra Day O'Connor, Ruth Bader Ginsberg, Maya Angelou, and Beverly Sills; and the presence of articulate older feminists such as Eliza-

EXERCISE 2

Honoring Your Glorious Age

As you settle into your present age, reflect on and respond either in your imagination or in action to the following questions. Do this alone or with a group of women.

1. Now that you have reached this glorious age, what do you wish to tear up?
2. What do you wish to give away?
3. What do you wish to burn?
4. What do you wish to remove?
5. Now that you have reached this glorious age, what do you wish to plant?

beth Janeway, Betty Friedan, and Gloria Steinem, have all empowered today's Jubilee women to cross its threshold with elan.
"Isn't she great?" we find ourselves remarking to one another of
intriguing older women, implying, "I can be like that too."

Another factor easing the passage is the creativity older
women are now expressing more freely. In particular, much
creative energy is being poured into ceremonies that either
combat and resist negative stereotypes about aging or advance
positive ones. Irene Fine, a Jewish woman who gathers such
ceremonies, records several that describe positive ways to enter

6. What do you wish to sing?
7. What do you wish to create?
8. What do you wish to wear?

If you're doing this exercise in a group, ask for a volunteer
who has recently passed over or soon will cross over the
threshold of another birthday. Together, prepare a ritual in-
corporating responses to the questions asked above as they
apply to her experience. Include gestures and actions of
tearing up, giving away, burning, removing; planting,
singing, creating, wearing.

If you are doing this exercise alone, prepare a ritual in-
corporating your responses to these questions, recording
them in your journal, and enacting them for yourself in
honor of the glorious age you have attained.

the passage signified by Jubilee's threshold. Plant a tree and say, "I plant this tree so that its roots will mingle with my ashes, and those of you who come after me will be blessed in its shade," to affirm that you maturely accept the reality of death. Wear a special garment or piece of jewelry belonging to a grandmother or woman elder in your life. Give out S.O.W. awards to all the Salty Old Women present at an elder's birthday ceremony. Fine says that actions such as tearing up, giving away, burning, or removing can have cathartic ritual value too. Exercise 2 is appropriate for whatever Jubilee age we are venerating.

Some women ease the passage by ritually crossing the Jubilee threshold every day. Marie, a California musician who is 71, told me that though she's aware of the motto "Today is the first day of the rest of my life," she's chosen another one as she moves through the land of aging. As she awakes and starts each day, she breathes the mantra "Today is my life" instead. Velma, a thoughtful 65-year-old Canadian, reported she'd learned from a ritual of Canada's native peoples to greet each day by stepping into it psychically and physically. "Most mornings," she said, "I gather myself and then consciously step into the day; I step into the world; I step into myself. Then after each step, I pause to become aware." In her stepping, she's intuitively recognized the historical connections linking the threshold, threshing (something done with the feet), and crossing a doorsill (something over which a person steps).

Such practices as these may be simple, but they're powerful too. By physically enacting them, we directly confront the passage of age. By spiritually affirming them, we move past age resistance and into a vision of every threshold we cross as another possibility for entering the fullness of life.

A STORE OF WISDOM

We do not enter the land of Jubilee Time as blank slates. Instead, we bring with us a rich store of wisdom built up from many previous thresholds and passages. As older women, we carry innumerable insights into later life, drawn from personal experience and from observing women who've preceded us. Exercise 3, below, helps us probe some of this wisdom.

After pausing to meditate on these questions and to record

EXERCISE 3

Uncovering Wisdom

Before reading the following pages, pause to meditate on your responses to three questions. After concentrating on your breathing and becoming quiet, take a few moments with each.

1. What is something you know now that you didn't when you were younger?
2. What is something life has taught you about age and aging?
3. Describe an incident or the circumstances that accompany your learnings. Did your wisdom come all at once or grow slowly over time?

your answers to them, compare them with the following responses I received when I asked these questions.

"Life is a series of letting go's. Each new stage has its own birthing with the joys and pains that follow," affirmed one woman. Said another, "The recesses of the psyche are wonderful sometimes but horrid too." A 53-year-old woman who directs twelve-step programs was more personal. "I know now," she wrote, "that I am an alcoholic. Knowing that, I also know the more I truly embrace my disease, the healthier and freer I become."

Regina, a 63-year-old university professor, offered this wisdom: "Something I know? Most things are not as important as we think and some far more." Judith, a 52-year-old ordained minister, referred directly to the theme of passage. "I know now *everything* passes. I can tell people they will make it, get through whatever difficulty they're experiencing."

Often, women seemed to have learned the same lessons, but expressed them in different ways. As the first part of life ended, many realized that although we have responsibilities *to* the rest of the universe, we are ultimately responsible *for* ourselves. No one else is in charge of our lives. One woman put it in the simplest terms: "I know I am responsible for me." "I have choices," another elaborated, "and I'm responsible for those choices. In fact, all that I *need* I *already* have." My 72-year-old neighbor, Catherine, phrased it this way: "We create our own reality," while Bernadette, 60, mused, "I've learned that I have a right to be here. Learning this has taught me that's true of everyone else too. All people and things have this right. It's as if I've come home at last."

Another common theme was finally understanding that the core of life is spiritual, not material. "Life has taught me," said Helen at 70, that "all is gift and my response is to be open to receive." She tied this directly to the discovery that "my dark nights were the greatest graces God ever gave me." Mary, describing an "increasing freedom to be myself," reported that at 62, she now knows "that one must take time to savor life; that God is very close."

Sixty-six-year-old Mary Lou reported, "I know everything is in a state of change, and miracles happen. There is something in life that is living *me*." That testimony to continuing change—and the wisdom it brings—can be read as a comment on thresholds. We continue to meet them, surprised by the miracle of new beginnings throughout our lives. In *The Measure of My Days,* a memoir she wrote in her eighties, Jungian analyst Florida Scott-Maxwell expresses her wonder at this dynamic.

Age puzzles me. I thought it was a quiet time. My seventies were interesting, and fairly serene, but my eighties are passionate. I grow more intense as I age. To my surprise I burst out with hot conviction. Only a few years ago I enjoyed my tranquility; now I am so disturbed by the outer world and by human quality in general that I want to put things right as though I still owed a debt to life. I must calm down. I am far too frail to indulge in moral fervour.

THRESHOLDS IN JUBILEE TIME

When we count seven years of seven years and enter Jubilee Time we can expect to face several major thresholds. Each has the potential to do more than alter or change our material circumstances. It becomes an opportunity to explore new spiritual territory, revealing a sacred calling to the next steps along the path. Although our individual thresholds will be as unique and varied as we are, common ones are *reengagement* (a better word than *retirement*), *loss, unfinished personal business,* and *the decades.*

Reengagement

In the 1950s and 1960s, gerontologists were fond of using the word *disengagement* to describe what they perceived to be a central component in aging. Growing older was assumed to be an inevitable process of severing or altering relationships, and was equated with moving away from life, loosening our hold on it, letting it go. The older we got, the more we were expected to withdraw from ordinary human involvement. As people lived longer and became both more self-aware and more vocal, however, it became clear we didn't disengage as a matter of course. Attention shifted from the threshold of disengagement to the threshold of retirement.

But *retirement* doesn't completely name what happens, either, once we move our energies away from work or a paid job to other pursuits. Instead, the change in circumstances that characterizes mature adult life today—which may include retirement—is most accurately described as *reengagement.* As one woman told me, "I'm never retiring. I'm just changing my activities."

This is true for Frances, an African-American nurse who stopped salaried work at 70 and took up travel overseas for three years, following that with a full-time ministry in her church when she finally settled back home. It's true for Louise, my 63-year-old sister-in-law, who now easily refuses once-seductive invitations to give "just a few days" to her former company as its resident computer expert, preferring to "read, read, read," take advantage of Elderhostel, and study Shakespeare. "I'm hungry to learn," she told me. "The kids have finished college, and finally I have the chance." Edna, 76, agrees there's plenty to engage us. "We can still be part of the kind of work we once did if we want to, but we have more choice in our activities. We can do home improvements we've postponed, we can learn new crafts."

Other women report they've discovered reengagement with other people as their working days have ended, and found gatherings of other women to be sources of new involvement. Katherine, 76, says it took her a long time to realize this. "Even after my retirement from a full-time job, I went along, living each day as it came with no awareness of any change except in my place of residence and type of activity—the kind of adjustments I've been making most of my adult life." But then, she reports, she suddenly had to have major surgery and, with the increasing decline in her physical energy, began to draw on the strengths of others. "I came to accept the fact," she concluded, that "we're all tied up together in the 'bundle of life' and our interdependence fills existence with much more meaning."

Actually, most women I polled reported that work of some kind remained part of their lives, but their attitudes toward it changed. This contributed to their re-creating new living styles, free of pressure and ambition.

I'm still doing lots of accounting and record keeping, but life is even more fulfilling and meaningful without the pressures of a career and social obligations relating to business and role expectations. (Mary, 71)

The pressure to excel is off. I feel free to be myself, to please myself instead of trying to meet the expec-

A Guided Meditation on Retirement

Before considering the threshold of loss, take time to uncover your feelings, expectations, and understandings of retirement—whether you are still on the job, recently retired, or well into a period of reengagement. Begin by attending to your breathing, inhaling and exhaling on the word *retire*. When you have quieted down and centered, close your eyes and imagine the following situations.

1. It is the first day of your retirement. Picture yourself on awakening and becoming aware that this day stretches before you, to do with as you choose. See yourself as you lie in bed. How do you feel? How long do you stay there? What options does the day hold for you? Which ones, if any, do you choose? When you get up, what time is it?
2. You go to the closet. What clothes do you select? What clothes do you consciously decide against? What shoes—if any—do you put on?

tations of others. . . . I can get by on my small income; I don't have any money or property to worry about. And although I'm involved in community activities, I now decline to take leadership responsibility. (Mel, 77) (See Exercise 4.)

3. What do you prepare for breakfast? *Do* you prepare or do you skip it? Does someone else bring it to you to celebrate the occasion? Do you turn on the television? The radio? A CD?

4. The phone rings. Who is calling? What do they have to say? After listening, you tell them this is the first day of your retirement. They ask you what it holds for you. What do you answer? Take time listening to yourself as a partner in the conversation and imagining yourself as you speak.

5. In your imagination, move ahead ten years. Imagine the same four moments: awakening, dressing, preparing breakfast, the phone call alerting you to consider your retirement. What, if anything, do you repeat from your earlier experience? What is different now? How are *you* different?

6. Finally, imagine the actual day stretching before you. What do your plans for it reveal to you about how you're living in relation to retirement?

7. Conclude with a return to consciousness of your breath, and to breathing the word *retire.*

Women reported that the elasticity of time now theirs and
its slower pace brought them face-to-face with the poignancy
of growing older. One 78-year-old agreed it was "great the
buck doesn't stop here anymore—at least, for the first ten years
after retirement it was great. But the older years I'm just beginning to face do not look so good. As long as I could func-
tion similarly to my old patterns, I liked aging. Now, I'm not
so sure." She's realizing that in addition to reengagement, Jubilee Time inevitably beckons us to cross a second major
threshold—loss. That loss may take many forms: mental failure,
physical impairment, disease, the loss of our homes. Here, we
examine the most universal: losing a beloved person.

THE LOSS OF A LIFE PARTNER

In a lovely and touching song, "No Tears for the Widow," Australian vocal artist Judy Small reminds us that the second half of
life, with its accumulation of years, presents a unique threshold—the loss to death of someone who has been a beloved and
intimate partner on life's journey over an extended period of
time, someone with whom we've planned to grow old. None of
us is immune: eventually, such loss cuts across all of our lives.

I think, for example, of my mother, who became a widow
too early, at 41. I was always aware how the sorrow of my father's death scarred her life. But I never realized the depth human grief could reach until the day her younger sister died
suddenly. By then my mother was 76; Helen—her "little sister"
and closest friend—was 73. They'd shared a lifetime of secrets,
delights, travel, and pain, including their mother's death when
they were children and the death of Helen's 27-year-old
daughter. All her previous losses failed to prepare my mother

for that grief, which remained a permanently open wound. But it also impelled her into new friendships with other women and made her feel comfortable with and even welcoming toward her own death sixteen years later.

I think too of Jean, a close friend who was an executive secretary to the CEO of a large business for twenty-three years. Jean had her own family, her own beloved spouse and children, as did Sam, her boss. But the two were a perfect professional team who delighted in each other's company and each other's work. The impact of Sam's death at 55 took a life partner from Jean, who was ten years his senior. Though most people didn't acknowledge her grief—she wasn't "family"—*she* did. After a pause to mourn, she dealt with the loss creatively, gathering Sam's papers and finding within herself the strength to leave the path of that partnership and begin a new career as a writer.

I think of innumerable older lesbian partners—the "widows" for whom there are no tears in Judy Small's song—whose grief is granted little or no public sanction except by their closest friends. I think too of a 70-year-old woman I loved in my childhood. Even then I knew she was mistress to a dying married lover. Though not living with his wife, he'd never divorced her, and when he died, Bea's loss went unacknowledged. Each of these women had to cross an agonizing threshold and desperately needed time for mourning, support from friends and family, and recognition of her sorrow.

Still, the women who have experienced the death of a marriage partner give us the most extensive understanding of such loss, perhaps because their voices are most often heard, most publicly respected. It is hard to be unmoved by the simple eloquence of the comment one seventy-year-old made in naming the worst thing about growing older: "The death of my husband: an amputation leaving a hurt, a scar."

"Becoming a widow at the age of 55," was Elizabeth's immediate response to the same question. "Growing older while being left a widow is scary. The word *widow* is a very big word to me. It holds so many responsibilities." Yet one positive effect of crossing this threshold has been her discovery, as it was for the women cited earlier, "that I am responsible for my life; that I am more capable of doing things on my own."

Gloria's husband died suddenly three and a half years ago. For her that's meant "adjustment to a single life, no one to share in the decision making, and the loneliness and sadness of being alone as I grow older." Now, at 65, she reflects on the new life taking shape within her. "Not only am I growing older physically, but mentally as well. I'm finding maturity in learning to take care of myself first, and giving over the responsibility of life to my children, free from me." She concludes, "I feel comfortable; peaceful; and glad to be retired, to enjoy travel, relationships, family, in my time and at my pace; free to make decisions about my welfare and life. I feel a serenity."

Sometimes we are prepared for the threshold of loss. May Sarton's journals, for example, detail the long waiting time between the initial sporadic forgetfulness of her beloved friend, Judy, and the eventual deterioration that led to Judy's death. Visiting her friend after a hiatus of several months, May describes the visit in words that reflect many women's experience of loss. "There she was, there she will be until she slips away, in her wheelchair, singing to herself. I know now that she will not recognize me, but I held her cold little hand and talked about old times."

UNFINISHED PERSONAL BUSINESS

The busyness of life's early decades, particularly for women, often precludes our tending to ourselves. At one of the first Jubilee retreats I led, one woman described a moment that had occurred four days after she was married, but that had consequences lasting over thirty years.

"I can still vividly see myself on that day," she reported. "People were calling me by my new name, Mrs. Covington. I didn't realize then I had other options, and I recall saying to myself, 'Mitzi, you've become someone else. You've got to put the Mitzi you've known all your life into a drawer now, and shut that drawer.' And I did. That day, very consciously, I imagined myself opening a large bureau drawer, pulling it out, and placing myself inside. Then I shut it. But now," she concluded, "I'm 53. I'm returning to her. I've got business to transact with her, parts of myself to reconcile with the person I'm becoming in my Jubilee years."

Since that day, other women have told me similar stories. As they begin dwelling in Jubilee Time, something alerts them to parts of themselves forgotten or unknown or only now ready to emerge. They're hearing a call to cross the threshold and take care of business for which they're finally prepared.

Fern Reyna, a 55-year-old Native American of the Acoma tribe, the oldest continuously inhabited community in the United States, tells a story with striking parallels to Mitzi's. "In my youth/growing years, it was not good to be Indian, so I placed the Indian-me in the closet, to be forgotten for many years. A few years ago, I brought out the Indian-me, put it on with pride and love. However, I shed tears for the loss of my Indian youth."

Like Fern and like Mitzi, we rarely have to guess what business awaits us. It has a way of making itself known with time and circumstance, appearing as our own Jubilee revelation. Sometimes a great sorrow impels us. Joan, a successful businesswoman from Long Island, New York, says, "I began my fiftieth year—four years ago—feeling light and free. By then I'd learned not to fear death, after losing a 23-year-old daughter. There's a peacefulness about death I never felt before."

Then Joan continues, "The death of my daughter forced me to stop. In coming back anew I'm a much more spiritual

---

EXERCISE 5

Discarding the Locks

Upon entering our Jubilee years, we discover thresholds we must cross, although sometimes their crossing may be difficult. The doorways leading to them may have been locked—by circumstances, by lack of time, by ourselves, by life itself. In this exercise we work to open these locks. You'll need plain paper and crayons or colored pencils.

Begin by attending to your breath. When you have quieted down and become centered, respond to the following.

1.   Think of a threshold presently beckoning you that you fear or resist crossing.

person, and with all my pain, I'm a happier, deeper, more caring person than I was the first forty-nine years."

A community organizer who at 57 runs conferences and
seminars and does personal counseling, Ann spoke of recently
discovering parts of herself crying out for affection and com-
passion. "Up to now," she told me, "everyone's focus—including my own—has been on the public me. But now I'm
changing. I can't continue living without attending to the private, personal woman within me."

Many other women deliberately set out to rediscover

2. On plain paper, with crayons or with colored pencils,
   draw a representation of or symbol for this threshold.
3. Draw the doorway leading into this threshold.
4. Draw a lock and place it on the doorway.
5. Draw any other barriers that keep you from crossing
   this threshold.
6. Now draw a key that you know opens the lock.
7. Next draw yourself placing the key in the lock, turning
   it, and opening the door as wide as you can.
8. What do you see? What do you find? Is anyone waiting? If so, who?

Share your experience of this exercise with someone
who understands what it means to you to cross this
threshold.

this private person. Beginning her fiftieth year, Sheila talks of "the discovery that I carry within myself me at every age I've been so far. I didn't grow up evenly at every stage, so I carry these infant, baby, child, girl, adolescent, young career woman, new bride, young mother, wife of doctor, et cetera with me at all times."

Sheila describes how she intends to cultivate this realization. "There are parts of me from all these stages that I've hidden or denied because they weren't finished yet. But at this age, 49, I've discovered I don't need to ignore, silence, or reprimand these parts of myself. Instead I need to consider, listen to, and celebrate them. This gives me access to creativity, to my inner essence, and to my connection with the spark of God."

The circumstances of this inner work are essentially individual, though the work itself is universal. In our Jubilee years we discern an unspoken rule that each woman must interpret personally: whatever you put away or didn't develop when you were younger, you'll need to attend to now. The career woman who had her first child at 43 is at 50 raising a 7-year-old, something Mitzi did in her twenties and thirties. Women like Mitzi are now working outside their homes for the first time in decades and fulfilling themselves in other ways. As a general rule, our own personal muses and the unique circumstances of our lives will clue us in to what work awaits us. So will exercises such as "Discarding the Locks" on pages 22–23.

THE DECADES

The last thresholds I shall name are the decades, starting with our fifties and continuing through to our nineties, even our centennial. During these years, our inner elder makes herself known to us if we allow her to do so, and offers us the chance to cherish her existence as she accompanies us toward the end. (See Exercise 6.)

In our fifties, the inner elder is a companion who shelters our growing awareness of age, even as she puts up with our flirtations with age denial, when we ignore her or see her as an enemy. She encourages us as we learn not to take being alive for granted. She supports us as the first of our contemporaries die during this decade and we recognize physical changes in ourselves and our friends—in weight, hair, threats of cancer— that remind us of our mortality and force us to take better care of our bodies. First sporadically, and then more regularly, we slow our pace. We speculate about whether and when we should retire from our job or make a final job change. Guided by our inner elder, we circle the major Jubilee thresholds, scout and appraise them, and make regular forays across their borders. We are preparing to settle in the land of Jubilee for good.

In our sixties, we sense the presence of our inner elder supporting us as we put down roots in this land and take up permanent residence. We are no longer young and have come to value her companionship. We're becoming attuned to the fragility of time, especially the time we have left. Though we may not yet own, or feel we deserve the title Wise Woman, we do notice ourselves becoming ironic, unsurprised, and accepting of life's incongruities and mysteries. That irony strengthens us, even as we take ourselves less seriously, and ease our hold on being in control. We're also easing our hold on our adult children. On occasion, we may even pass up their invitations to spend holidays with them so we can be with our women friends or go to the Caribbean alone with our husband. We're

Befriending Our Inner Elder

Although many women have learned to cherish their inner child, who represents the childhood always present in them as part of their history, their inner elder is largely unknown. She represents the years and time of age that is also a part of the life cycle, and symbolically she dwells within each of us. This exercise provides an opportunity to meet and get to know her.

Begin by sitting quietly, centering, and breathing the phrase "inner elder." Breathing in, repeat the word *inner;* breathing out, repeat the word *elder.* When you have become calm, start with whatever decade you're in, and attend to the following questions as they apply to this decade of your life.

moving away from full involvement in our job or career and turning to other work that demands our attention, such as acting politically, cultivating rich interior gardens, or both.

Such work nourishes the passage into our seventies. In this decade, the hand of our inner elder, holding ours, grows stronger. By now our parents, and often our spouses, companions, sisters, and brothers, are gone, and death is a familiar presence. We've learned the delightful art of saying exactly what we think, and send the food back in restaurants without a tinge of regret if we don't like the way it's done. We're articulate and often involved in social issues too, although usually—but not always—we let other people run for office. Best,

1. Describe the woman who lives within you as your inner elder.
2. What is her name? Is it the same as yours, or does she bear a secret name known only to the two of you?
3. When is she happiest?
4. What frightens her most?
5. What gift do you sense she needs from you?
6. What gift does she offer you in return?

Imagine yourself holding a conversation with her and record your conversation in your journal, perhaps talking about your responses to these questions. When you have completed your conversation, conclude the exercise by returning to your breathing. Plan to return to the conversation with your inner elder at another time, meeting her as she appears in each of the decades following the present one.

despite growing physical complaints we feel unprecedented internal, spiritual freedom.

Crossing the threshold of the eighties, the inner and outer elder merge into one complete person. We appear more interesting to other people than we were in our seventies, and find ourselves amused by their attention. Sometimes we are passionate and aware, like Florida Scott-Maxwell; at other times we're unable to venture forth physically or mentally. In either case we tend to be gifted with peace. If we do pause to talk about being old, we're philosophical: "We all must face it," we say, or "I've no wish to be starting over," or "It's just a normal phase of life." We nod in agreement when we hear of 86-year-old Dame Judith Anderson, interviewed on her career in the theater. "We live, we breathe, we die, we love, we hate, we experience beauty and tragedy, and we find it in the parts we play." By the end of our eighties, we've played all the parts.

If and when we cross the threshold into our nineties and, even more, into a centennial birthday, death is very near, but so is life. We hold its fullness at our center, where the inner elder dwells. Often, her presence there is visible in our faces, and other people can see her. Together, we await what comes next. If our minds are gone or our mental life unexpressed, that may be all we are: sheer waiting. Waiting for immortality, eternity, resurrection, reincarnation, nothingness. Waiting for the moment of gathering and giving up all we've become. Waiting to pass over the last great threshold: from life into death.

Two

---

*T*HE *H*ALLOWING
OF *S*ABBATH

You shall keep a sabbath of complete rest. . . .

Lev. 25:4

On a day soon after we cross the threshold into Jubilee Time, we may be asked to start a magazine, run a bake sale, or organize a protest. We may be invited to chair a committee, oversee a building project, or lead a parade. We've demonstrated excellence at such things over the years and earned reputations as women who get the job done. But now, often for the first time in our adult lives, we say no.

We elaborate. "Of course I *could*. But for now, no."

We may go further. "No. I really can't."

Then, sometimes to our own surprise, we give the reason. "It's time for me to go apart and rest awhile."

TURNING INWARD

Saying no is a significant Jubilee moment. It symbolizes turning away from external demands on our time and acknowledging we have a right, even a duty, *not* to say yes to every request that comes our way. Despite occasional pangs of guilt for refusing someone, and periodic intrusions of "I *should* have said yes," stronger feelings prevail, based on the growing conviction that aging calls us to befriend an unfamiliar dimension of time: time set aside for not-acting, for stillness, for quiet.

Time for Hallowing.

The Hallowing of Sabbath is Jubilee's second ritual. To hallow means to make holy, to consecrate, to treat with reverence. To hallow means to hold someone or something sacred. To hallow means to set apart quiet moments for contemplation and receptivity. During Jubilee Time we pause for such contemplative quiet in order to hallow the second half of life.

The biblical foundation of this ritual is clear. As soon as we pass over Jubilee's threshold, we are to stop and savor time. "When you enter the land that I am giving you," says the God of Jubilee, "you shall keep a Sabbath of complete rest." After you've learned to do that, "you shall hallow the fiftieth year," honoring it as the entrance into that part of the life cycle when you say no to thoughtless activity and yes to mature spirituality.

When I was growing up in Jamaica, New York, in the 1930s and '40s, we didn't use the word *hallowing* in connection with spirituality. But we did learn to put aside special time to reverence the Mystery we called God. For good Catholic girls like me, that meant going to Mass, receiving Holy Communion, confessing my sins. For my Protestant friends, it meant participating in worship services, Sunday School, and Bible study. For my next-door neighbor Goldy Meresman, it meant attending temple, lighting the Sabbath candles, and gathering with family. For all of us it meant prayer. I remember noticing that for Goldy's mother, Fanny, her ritual Sabbath practices spilled over into providing gifts of food and warm conversation to the three of us who lived next door: my widowed mother, my brother, Tom, and me.

With age and experience, I've realized that people who engage in such practices hold two quite different attitudes toward spirituality. Those with the first withdraw periodically from ordinary life because the world is sinful, even evil. Spirituality equals piling up "holy" acts that get us through the "unholy" ones such as wiping children's bottoms, doing laundry, and taking out the garbage. The more we distance ourselves from matter and flesh, the easier our path to the Divine Spirit and the unseen world.

Those with the second attitude assume the opposite: we pause for rituals of Hallowing in order to remember and acknowledge the goodness of the world and its lavish, generous Creator. Intervals of complete rest remind us of the stillness accessible in all our days. Attending to the Divine Spirit during special moments reminds us of that Spirit's hovering presence during all life's moments. Dwelling in the holiness of Sabbath time returns us refreshed to the holiness of ordinary time.

The second attitude guides us in Jubilee Time. By the age of 50, most of us have learned to suspect as flawed any spirituality that dismisses what's daily and commonplace. Still assigned the human tasks of cleaning, cooking, and caring that keep us in touch with life's basics, we women know that the simple routines of life are sacred trusts, and the simple rhythms of day and night are good. We're leery of a this-world-versus-other-world spirituality, and instead of repeating sour cautions such as "Watch out: you can get too much of a good thing," we're much more likely to intone Mae West's credo: "Too much of a good thing is wonderful!" (See Exercise 1.)

EXERCISE 1

Donning the Mantle of Jubilee

This exercise is designed to help you embody and express willingness to enter the ritual of Hallowing. It can be done alone or with others.

Preliminary: Search your wardrobe for a garment—perhaps a shawl or scarf, perhaps a special sweater or a cloak—that is a fitting symbol to associate with your Jubilee years. It may be something of your own, or it may have belonged to an influential woman in your life: older sister, mother, daughter, grandmother, good friend, great-aunt, teacher.

If necessary, clean the garment with care. Iron or block it, making it as hallowed as possible.

1. Begin the exercise by sitting down and placing the garment around your shoulders.

Fifty-three-year-old Cynthia, who'd been brought up to believe that evading pleasure, denying herself, and hiding her sexuality were spiritual centerpieces, agreed. During a Jubilee retreat I led, she told me she'd already realized her spirit's work was getting rid of "the stuff" around such negative ideas, "becoming aware of and confronting this stuff so I can find God everywhere, in everyone, at every moment."

2. Gently hold the edges of the garment with both your hands.
3. Sit still and wordlessly for a full five minutes, attending to your breath as you inhale and exhale. Feel yourself relaxing.
4. After five minutes, respond to the following, putting your answers in a notebook for future reflection.
   a) What is one thing about your age you want to bless?
   b) What is one thing about your age you want to study?
   c) What is one thing about your age you want to reject?
   d) Who is one older person you choose to hallow as a model for aging?
   e) What ordinary moment in your life do you want to hallow daily?
5. Conclude the practice by repeating a phrase such as "Today I take on Jubilee as my garment" or "This is the garment of my Hallowing."

THE MYSTICAL DIMENSION

Though she may not have realized it, Cynthia was singing the song of the mystic: everyone and everything is connected with everyone and everything else, and all's filled with divinity, aflame with the grandeur of God. Any moment can be a sacred moment that knocks us onto our knees in adoration and wonder. But if we never stop to consider that or to say yes to its possibility, we're in danger of missing it. To nourish such attentiveness, we have to slow down; we have to set aside time; we have to practice stillness and quiet—ironically by saying a regular, ritual no. Jubilee introduces such hallowing with the command:

> When you enter the land that I am giving you, the land shall observe a sabbath for the Lord. Six years you shall sow your field, and six years you shall prune your vineyards, and gather in their yield; but in the seventh year there shall be a sabbath of complete rest. (Lev. 25:2–4)

That Jubilee teaching prescribes rest for all living things: when *you* stop sowing and pruning and reaping, the impact of such a creative pause flows over to anyone who works for you, to your children, to strangers in the area, to animals, and to the earth itself. Hallowing has implications far beyond ourselves.

As a ritual for Jubilee women, Hallowing begins when we heed the summons to bless the coming of age by keeping a personal Sabbath. That Sabbath eventually impels us to look beyond ourselves to the earth, and let its land lie fallow. Finally, from the deep centers of stillness these practices create within us, we rekindle forgotten or unused capacities for thick listening, prayerful awareness, and compassionate care.

SABBATH

Sabbath is primary ground in the ritual of Hallowing, just as it is the fundamental pause, stop, and no-saying in Western spirituality. For the ancient Babylonians, *sappatu* meant "the time for quieting the heart," and the Hebrew *shavat* means "cessation" or "desistance" from work. Judaism has always made it clear, however, that the cessation and desistance are not pessimistic. Instead, Sabbath's turning away from labor, striving, and anxiety is positive and holy. Out of Sabbath's not-doing, a richer, more bountiful kind of doing emerges.

Long before I found Jubilee, I taught about Sabbath. Often, my students were puzzled when I introduced them to its Zenlike character. They'd come up to me after class with notepads and pens in hand, earnestly begging me to tell them what a person *did* during Sabbath. "It's a not-doing," I'd answer, feeling like a bodhisattva. "But what do we *do* during the inactivity?" they'd press. "What are the rules?"

At that point, I'd find myself recalling a story a friend brought back from Kyoto. The story was in the form of a dialogue between a student and a teacher.

> *Student:* If the Buddha is more than Siddhartha Gotama, who lived many centuries ago, then tell me, please, what is the real nature of Buddha?
> *Teacher:* The blossoming branch of a plum tree.

Student: What I asked, worthy teacher, and what I am
    eager to know is, what is the Buddha?
Teacher: A pink fish with golden fins swimming idly
    through the blue sea.
Student: Will not your reverence tell me what the Bud-
    dha is?
Teacher: The full moon, cold and silent in the night sky,
    turning the dark meadow to silver.

That was the entire story. It stayed with me because, like the
Zen master, I was trying to show the students they'd asked an
unanswerable kind of question. Rather than depend on me,
they needed to turn to their own experience, whether that was

EXERCISE 2

Turning to the Mystery

A *mantra* is a word or a short phrase that centers us when it
is repeated. In this practice, you choose a mantra to symbolize your desire to be in the presence of the Hallowed
One at creation's center.

Some of you will wish to choose a name for the Holy
(Goddess, Mother, Friend, etc.) as a mantra; others will signal turning to that Presence by a word such as *hallow* or
Sabbath. The phrase "no word" may even serve as mantra,
as will a simple syllable such as *om*. Once we choose, we
turn to this Mystery by practicing three steps:

of plum trees, the blue sea, or the dark meadow. I knew they'd find Sabbath by embracing and entering it.

My cryptic responses eventually conveyed to these earnest neophytes that Sabbath's not-doing means entering a kind of not-knowing or even unknowing, a soul-place where the too-hurried pace of life slows down and another way of walking beckons, one characterized by prayerfulness and awe. They became alert to the belief that not-doing in the way Sabbath suggests is a key that unlocks another world. Once they understood that, they found specific ways to observe Sabbath on their own.

Jubilee women's entrance into Sabbath begins with turning to the Mystery, the Holy One at the center of creation,

1. Sit comfortably, gently releasing inner and outer hurry. Close your eyes and spend three to five minutes coming to awareness of your breath. Breathe in; breathe out. Inhale; exhale. Feel your whole self becoming less pressured; feel your whole self becoming receptive.

2. When you are quieted, silently speak the word/phrase you've chosen to signify your turn to the Mystery. As you breathe in, repeat it calmly, slowly; then breathe out. Do this for five minutes.

3. Conclude by making a physical gesture—upraised hands, deep bow, turn to the four directions—as a recognition of the Sacred Mystery at the center of the universe and at the center of your hallowing.

however we might name that One: Yahweh, the Unnameable, or simply "Thou." Sabbath serves as the primary sacrament reminding us of this mysterious presence everywhere, including in our midst. When we become still and quiet, we foster encounter with It, and in the meeting learn to let go, give up control, and trust ourselves to this Presence. (See Exercise 2.)

While Sabbath rest reverences the Mystery, it is also something we do for ourselves. Rest rescues us from going into overdrive or burning out, ceaselessly working to get things done. Sixty-four-year-old Teddy told me, "As I began to grow older, I stopped helping God get the sun up every day and paint the sunset every evening, though it took me a while to accept God's ability to handle those things alone. When I did, I found time to sit still and simply be." Such rest creates zones of quiet where the arts of hallowing tutor us.

Yet it also impels us beyond ourselves, and rightly so, because we actually have a *capax universi,* a capacity for the universe. If we don't make outer journeys to those who might need us, along with our inner ones, we get spiritually sick. That is part of Sabbath wisdom too. For although it starts as a ceremonial command to imitate and honor a Creator God who rested when the world was done, it becomes moral and ethical by the time it is recorded in the book of Exodus. There Sabbath rest must be granted to strangers, prisoners, animals, and the land itself. In a strange reversal, turning inward for not-doing makes our worlds larger, not smaller.

"Remember the sabbath day and keep it holy. Six days you shall labor and do all your work. But the seventh day is a sabbath to your God; on it you shall not do any work," the command begins. But then it continues, as it does later in the Book of Leviticus, "You shall not do any work—but not only you.

Don't demand labor from your son or daughter, your male or female slave, your livestock, the alien resident in your towns, or the stranger at your gates" (Exodus 20:8). As with all genuine spirituality, Sabbath rest occurs in the center of the community, where it equalizes human beings and undercuts the temptation to "use" anyone or anything—whether that's another person, an animal, or a tree. We aren't even permitted to use— or let others use—ourselves.

LET THE LAND LIE FALLOW

Following Sabbath rest, the ritual of Hallowing directs us to let the land lie fallow. The land is our mother; the land is our sister. But most of all, the land is our home. Earth holds in its body our personal stories and those of our ancestors. Earth holds the ashes and remains of those we've loved and lost to death. Earth keeps us alive, offering us air to breathe, water to drink, food to eat. Earth greets us when we're born, and receives us back into herself when we die. Earth is a role model for God.

We're latecomers to this planet Earth, which had a fully developed biosphere 180 million years ago. Our relative immaturity may be one reason why, at a global level, we've only recently become aware of the life-and-death crisis facing our mother/sister/home. Theologian and award-winning writer Beth Johnson points out that a mere forty thousand years ago, bands of us roamed as hunter-gatherers. Ten thousand years ago we lived in rural farm villages; five thousand years ago we formed cities and invented writing; two hundred years ago we devised steam engines and started the industrial revolution.

Conversing with the Earth

Before reading any further, pause to interact with one element of the earth, in order to hallow your relation to it and your responsibility to let it lie fallow. Where possible, hold the actual element in your hand—a fistful of soil; a tumbler of water; the branch of a tree; the feeling of your breath. Then do the exercise, which is in the form of a conversation.

You may want to record the conversation in your journal, or you may decide to hold it silently and meditatively in your imagination.

1. Choose a symbol of one of the major elements in creation—earth (dirt, soil, wood, flower, vegetable); water (ocean water, tap water, rain, snow, ice); air (wind, hurricane, breeze, your breath); fire (flame, sun, summer heat).
2. Sketch or draw the symbolic element you've chosen as a way to sharpen your encounter and to "hold" it.
3. Introduce yourself and ask the element a question. Then give the element a voice so that it can respond.

But thirty years ago, our numbers began to multiply out of proportion to other living species and to the earth's carrying capacity. Now, she writes, "the smoldering ecological crisis [has] blazed into a firestorm. The water, air and soil are being rapidly depleted, and all other living things are finding

You can be sure that if you're relaxed and attentive, the conversation will flow from there.

Sample beginnings:

You: (*Scooping up particles of dirt from outside and holding them in your hand*) "How are you this morning, Sister Earth?"

Earth: "How do I seem to you?"

You: "I'll have to pause and take some notice. Let me see what strikes me particularly about you right now. . . ."

or

You: (*Holding an apple*) "Thank you for resting in my hand."

Apple: "You're welcome. I'm glad to be here."

You: "I'm wondering how you've been treated from the time you grew on the tree until now."

Apple: "Would you like me to tell you about that?"

You: "Yes, I think that will help me let the land lie fallow."

Apple: "Well, in the beginning . . ."

Conclude the conversation after fifteen or twenty minutes.

life more difficult, if not impossible." That's due to us, the latecomers.

In the midst of this situation, the biblical command once translated by some as "subdue" and "dominate" the earth reemerges as an urgent plea to "befriend" and "dress" her. We must walk tenderly across her valleys and plains as we make the land a daily companion in our spirituality.

How we might do this was the focus of an interview I had with a 75-year-old Benedictine sister. We were talking about the ecological consciousness taking root around the planet today, and the proposal by many environmentalists that Francis of Assisi be the patron of the ecological movement because of his reverence toward creation.

In our conversation, Sister reminded me passionately that reverence is not enough—especially today. "Wherever we go," she said with intensity, "we interact with the earth and its creatures, through technology and lifestyles and the ways we carry on agriculture. Our footprints mark the places we walk, even if our walk is gentle."

Then, referring to her own tradition, she proudly said, "Centuries ago, you may know, Benedictines, women and men, realized we were part of an ecosystem, and as farmers, builders, and scholars we transformed soil, water, plants, and animals by listening to them carefully, and then responding to what they were telling us. We didn't use destructive chemicals or burn forests or exhaust the soil by overplanting. That's the way we let the land lie fallow today—by putting reverence and responsibility, listening and responding together."

Growing older helps us recover such hallowing attitudes. Just as our aging bodies aren't infinitely resilient and often feel depleted, so too with the earth's body—our aging mother isn't infinitely productive or an endless source of resources either. The women of our planet demonstrate a remarkable sensitivity to this: in northern India women hug the trees to save them; in Kenya women who are part of the Greenbelt movement plant trees while "developed nations" send bulldozers to tear them up. Japanese "Fuji Grannies" camp out trying to stop industrial building around Mt. Fuji. When arrested they say, "We're not making any trouble here. We're too old."

That kind of passionate responsibility to the earth relates intimately to responsibility for the earthly creation we are, especially as we age. It nags us to consider the destructiveness of many of our diets—not only ceaseless and repeated diet*ing,* but the abusive ways we starve ourselves of genuine nutrition. We can restore practices of healthy eating by taking time to let the land of our own flesh lie fallow, attending to habits of bodily care beyond the purely cosmetic. These might include walking daily, moderating alcohol use, eliminating fat from our diets, and increasing our intake of fruits and vegetables, especially those with calcium and potassium, both important to post-menopausal women.

Let the land lie fallow. Unless we're willing to be still, to withdraw from work periodically, to rest in the way Sabbath teaches, we will be unable to save ourselves. We will be unable to save one another. We will be unable to save our planet. Ironically, this rest and reverence is an essential ingredient in all the more active rituals that follow: Freedom, Journey, Inventory, Story, and Gratitude. So are Hallowing's three other steps: thick listening, prayerful awareness, and compassionate care. (See Exercise 3.)

THICK LISTENING

Our ordinary patterns of listening are often thin. We pay minimal attention to the flotsam and jetsam of daily life. But certain signals—for example, the tone of our daughter's voice carrying just the slightest urgency as she drops in for a visit and then says, "Mom, I want to ask you something"—prompt a shift to the intuition "Uh-oh. Something here needs my complete attention." Our thick listening is activated.

We begin our lives listening thickly, attentive to all the sounds of our environment, usually so much so that we need shelter from them. Noise that is too loud, too frequent, or too intense can be damaging to an infant, who, like us even now, needs an atmosphere of Sabbath quiet.

Eventually we learn to identify the important, life-giving sounds—the voices of our parents, the preparation of food, the summons of special music. The capacity to recognize these sounds demands a listening that carries within it a basic silence, the silence residing *in* the listening, like water in a sponge. Without such silence, thick listening goes flat, and as we grow older and more verbal, we may even impede it. For example, instead of listening thickly to other people while they speak, we use the time to ready a response we'll make when they're through.

Some of us never lose the original listening capacity: we're the ones echoing the wise woman who says of herself, "Sometimes ah sets and thinks, 'n sometimes ah jes sets." More typically, however, life's pace and the omnipresent din of stereo and television inside the house and motors, horns, and boom boxes outside (especially if we live in the city) deaden our listening, make us poor at it—at worst, incapable of it. Demands for our physical presence eat away at once-strong powers of spiritual presence. The best we can manage is hiding out in the bathroom, or taking infrequent, all-too-quick pauses from life's routines when, briefly, we catch our soul's breath.

With the Jubilee years, however, earlier listening capacities reappear. We are often alone. The natural Sabbaths of Jubilee that cause our bodies to slow down calm our spirits too. Hallowing the decades of life's second half provokes us to set aside interior fallow periods.

During these intervals, as our spirits lie quiet and we accept the summons to rest, we turn to earlier or unused listening practices we may have forgotten. We pause to identify the changing rain patterns in a storm; we make music foreground, not background, and sit still for it, engaged as it plays. We also recapture our childhood capacity for intense listening. Just as little children pick up more from grown-ups' tone of voice, posture, and facial expression than from their actual words, so the wisdom of age, the movement as elders to the periphery of conversations, and the more relaxed pacing of our days alert us to unheard voices and unspoken wishes. Taught by experience that people "speak" in innumerable ways, we match their body language with their verbal language and listen to their whole person.

Such thick listening may come naturally. But more commonly, it comes because we cultivate it. Answering the Sabbath command to keep a complete rest, we eventually realize that thick listening arises when we periodically cease activity, choose a special place, and set apart minutes, hours, and days for it. Fifty-six-year-old Joyce agreed. "I've grown to love walking by myself anywhere—city, ocean, or country. It helps my serenity and prayer, not to mention my body!"

Other women I've met are more deliberate, describing practices that both slow them down and intensify their listening.

I take time each day to meditate in the morning. And I must read before bed at night. I also take time to stand at

my window or outside if possible, to greet the day in the
morning and to greet the night. I'm also learning things

EXERCISE 4

A Pattern for a Day of Thick Listening

9:00   Unplug the phone or take it off the hook; unplug
the television.

Choose a place in your home that you will hallow
as your meditation spot: a chair you put on a special
rug, a part of a room, a section of your porch.

When you are settled, choose a mantra for the day,
one you've used before or one you create for this one
day. Spend twenty minutes listening to your breath, repeating the mantra as a way to orient the day.

9:30 Walk, run, or sit outdoors, gardening or listening to
the earth. Try painting or sketching anything that
catches your attention or seems to be speaking to
you.

If the weather keeps you indoors, attend to one or
several of your plants, works of art, or other objects and
paint or sketch them.

10:30   Break for a cup of tea, cocoa, or coffee. Drink it
slowly, attending to each sip.

10:45   Choose a book you've been meaning to read, or
choose a selection of music you've been intending

for enjoyment—yoga, Reiki, the Goddess in our lives,
Native American and Wiccan spirituality. (Eileen at 54)

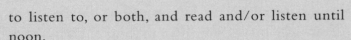

to listen to, or both, and read and/or listen until
noon.

12:00 Write a letter to yourself about why you're spending
this day as you are. Save it, dating it to be opened on
your next thick-listening day.

12:30 Eat lunch. Ideally, you have prepared this before-
hand. Set your place carefully, and treat yourself as you
might treat a cherished guest.

1:00 Lie down for an hour. Sleep if you can.

2:00 Get up and again walk or sit outdoors, this time not
only listening to but conversing with the earth, as you
did in exercise 3.

2:45 Move your listening from the earth and direct it to
the Mystery at the center of the universe. Choose a
psalm from the Bible, or Leviticus 25, or a favorite
poem or prayer, and imagine the words as the voice of
the Mystery. What are the words saying? What are they
saying *to you*?

3:30 In your journal or in a special retreat notebook,
write down your feelings and responses to the day as it
draws to a close. Write down what your listening has
enabled you to hear.

3:50 Close the day using your morning's mantra for ten
minutes as, once again, you attend to your breath.

As I go about the work of each day, I've learned not to rush things most of the time. It will all get done if it needs to, and it's more important to me that I don't feel pressured from within. (Phyllis at 57)

For me it's being conscious of my breath. And going to the mountains, as Psalm 122 says, "From whence shall come my help." (Kathleen at 50)

Still others include a daily fifteen-minute period of sitting still; weekly quiet hours; even monthly listening days, alone or in the company of others, often in a retreat setting. (See Exercise 4.)

The result of each of these is similar. Rather than feel guilt when compelled to say no, these women are shaping a spirituality for their later years that includes turning away from immediate external demands in order to turn inward and listen. That listening eventually creates an attitude of prayer that returns them refreshed and renewed to the world they call home.

PRAYERFUL AWARENESS

The practice of thick listening has a natural dynamic that eventually emerges into awareness, allowing us to perceive previously unnoticed facets of our lives. If we fast from radio and television for a day, for example, we catch music floating on other airwaves, like the sound of wind or the silence of snow.

If we pause for a five-minute mantra of *listen* before a meeting, we pick up nuances in our colleagues' voices that we generally miss. If we walk in slow motion at half our usual pace, even for ten minutes, we hear an inner voice that eludes us on more hurried occasions.

Because I'm a teacher, and have learned how crucial both listening and awareness are to learning, I've always been intrigued by how this happens, and the best description I've found comes from the philosopher Martin Buber. He names three possible ways to enter any situation. The first is to go in with a list of things to look for and questions to ask. This is the way my students first came to Sabbath, with pencils and paper in hand. Buber calls this the way of the observer.

In the second case, we bring no list. Instead, we trust our minds and hearts to pick up whatever's there. We're alert, interested, and inquisitive, and have faith we'll know "it" when we see it. Buber calls this the way of the onlooker. It's different in style from observing, but the two are similar in one crucial way: we still approach a situation as the actor, the agent, the one in control.

The third form of entry, called awareness, differs. It usually occurs during a reflective period of our lives, when we walk into a situation with the same attitude we bring to genuine prayer. We're not observers. We're not onlookers. We're not in charge. Instead, we're the ones observed and looked upon. We're the ones approached. Instead of doing the grasping, we're the ones who are grasped.

When we are, it is common to realize that something, perhaps even Someone, is addressing us, and instead of being initiators, we must respond. Perhaps a momentous decision awaits us. Perhaps we must quit our job, even our marriage. Perhaps we're being challenged to sell all our goods and give the proceeds to the poor. Alternatively, we may not know what we're supposed to do.

But in such a moment we do know a word demanding an answer is being spoken to us; a form of destiny is approaching us. We know we're being called into a deep awareness of who and what we are. In Jubilee Time, the "word demanding an answer" is age.

When we are merely observers of age, we get our paper and pencil and list what it's all about, even how to "do" it. When we're onlookers we're a bit closer, but we still keep some distance. We've not yet moved into befriending, embracing, and cherishing age. We've still got time—we imagine—to think about it.

But when we stand in the ritual of Hallowing and allow Jubilee's power to grasp us, we permit ourselves the possibility of deep, prayerful awareness. Here are some of the ways women have articulated their awareness of age to me.

I remember a day when I was reflecting on the fact that I was 50 years old. I suddenly saw the possibility that I still had half of my life to live. When I recalled all of the first fifty years, I was excited and challenged by the possibilities for the next fifty. My life has been just like that ever since—full of new possibilities all the time. So I feel excited and challenged. (Sarah, age 56)

With age I've become aware that other people bring assumptions about who I am to me, and I'm in danger of reacting to that, rather than being my actual self: someone constantly changing, open to what is new, not hemmed in by preconceptions or by an image of the woman I was when I was younger. (Vicki, age 54)

Ruth, a Canadian grandmother and graduate student in hospital administration, echoed Vicki, saying awareness of age for her is based on the conviction that finally "I can be myself. Because I am 'old' I no longer have to worry about what other people think." She continued, "After sixty-one years of doing and being what others want me to do or be, I can do what I want to do and be myself. My self-esteem has finally come to rest within me and not in externals."

Baba Copper also claims the word *old*. She is feisty about it, aware that to own age proudly turns prayerful awareness into political awareness too. In her powerful little book on aging, *Over the Hill,* she wryly testifies:

> I am an *old* woman. I am sixty-eight. Part of the reason I self-identify as *old* is a need to escape the prissy category of older. Calling myself an old woman was the radical way out . . . it may be presumptuous of me to assume a label which is descriptive of women in their nineties, but I have noticed that many of them avoid the term. Like other words which feminists are reclaiming by proud usage, I take to myself the word everyone seems to fear.

Other women describe the underside of age as part of their awareness: the threads on the reverse side of the tapestry that sometimes seem knotted or ugly. Some complain about feeling unproductive, superfluous, "no good to anybody." My friend Evelyn Whitehead interprets this underside more positively. In fact, she has a word for it—*uselessness*—and a conviction about its importance to spirituality. She says that throughout history, all the major religious traditions rebel against identifying people with their usefulness to society, and Buddhism and Taoism go even further. In those traditions, uselessness is a central spiritual category.

Evelyn tells the Taoist story of the woodsman who comes upon a massive, ancient tree. "At first sight it appears attractive to the woodsman. Upon closer examination, however, he realizes it's gnarled and so useless to him." But the point of the story, she says, lies in its irony. Its very uselessness guarantees the tree's continuing life and longevity.

Besides age and uselessness, the word *emptiness*—whether it refers to the empty womb of the postmenopausal years or the emptiness of a house without children, spouse, or companion—needs to be redefined for Jubilee Time. The experience of emptiness can serve as a time of crisis, which means it can be both a danger and an opportunity. If we give in to the view that emptiness is bad, we court the risk of despairing self-absorption. But if we read it as a signal that age empties our hands of previous commitments and frees them for others, emptiness can prepare us for Hallowing's last step. It can lead us to Care.

CARE

Care was walking along the river bank one day, picking up clumps of earth and thinking, "Wouldn't it be marvelous if human beings existed?" But because Care couldn't make humans, didn't have that power, Care sought help from the Sacred One walking nearby. She asked the Sacred One to take the clumps of earth and breathe life into them. And the Sacred One did.

Thus it came to pass that since the Sacred One had breathed life into us, It would receive us when we died; It was where we were going. Because we were made from the earth, from the humus, we would be called *human*. But because Care had thought of us in the first place, She would possess us all our lives. She would also possess *all* of our lives: their personal, social, political, and spiritual dimensions.

We've already encountered care for the land as we let it lie fallow. Concluding this ritual, we turn to care for one another, for society, and for ourselves.

The tendency to treat one another well is fragile; we have other, less noble tendencies. But we also have powerful pre-conscious and conscious memories of being cared for. One of the criteria for adults' dealing with childhood trauma is the memory of even one grown-up who affirmed and cared for us when we were little. Such memories help redeem uncared-for parts of ourselves, even as they bolster our adult efforts to care for others.

As younger women, we direct most of our care to our fam-ilies: children, spouse, aging parents. With our children, the bal-ance of care is usually on our part toward them. But children should practice care too; both boys and girls need to learn that care is part of the human vocation. For example, when my hus-band was a child, he spent his first six years as the youngest of four. But when his mother became pregnant with her fifth child, she schooled him in care. Throughout that pregnancy, she prepared him for the special role he would have as an older brother to the newborn, fragile infant who was coming, and be-stowed on him the responsibility to protect and care for his younger sibling. Fifty-two years later, the friendship between Gabriel and his sister Dotty is one of the most beautiful I know.

With age, as many of our care obligations diminish, we become increasingly free to widen our care circles, and to break down the public-private wall that sometimes separates parts of care from one another. If we have not done so as younger women, we now extend our care beyond the boundaries of family, neighborhood, class, and nation. That allows our caring to become a practice of planetary connectedness, where no one is too far away to receive our attention.

Such political involvement alerts us to institutions, systems, even laws that obstruct care, and compels us to work toward removal of political and social barriers that prevent it. Although born from a spirituality of quiet and hallowing that may at first seem entirely private, such involvement places acts of care at the center of public life too, reconciling "outer" and "inner" as any genuine spirituality must. Jubilee teaching holds that acts of care must include protest against unjust and killing debt, redistribution of resources such as land and capital, and the proclamation of freedom and works that serve justice, lived out by building houses through Habitat for Humanity, volunteering in shelters for homeless persons, and tending to the widow and her children, as Fanny Meresman did to my family. The no of Sabbath, quieting us into listening and awareness, eventually reemerges in the yes of responsibility and care.

As we age, we find the touchstone and test for the genuineness of our care lies in how we care for ourselves. If you are a "sandwich generation" woman who is taking care of her aged parents as well as her not-yet-adult children, you need respite from this daily caring. So you bring your parents to the local senior center for several hours a day. That senior center exists in a care circle with you because someone got politically involved in societal caring, realizing caregivers need care too.

EXERCISE 5

The Hands of Care

Sometimes we look at our hands only in terms of a manicure, or skin, or jewelry we might wear. This practice directs us to explore our hands as the primary means through which we express care.

1. Begin by tracing both of your hands on a sheet of paper, with palm side up.
2. On each of your fingers, name a way your hands have tended and continue to tend whichever of the following you wish to remember: another person; a nonhuman animal such as a cat or dog; the earth; yourself.
3. On the palm part of one hand, write—or draw an image for—how your hands express the care: giving a massage, extending a hug, watering a garden, drawing up a petition, etc.
4. On the palm part of the other hand, write—or draw an image for—what your hands express: sympathy, healing, protest, strength, etc.
5. Acknowledge and celebrate yourself as a caregiver by gently massaging your hands with oil or lotion, repeating the word *care* as you do, and breathing it as a mantra for at least five minutes as you conclude this exercise.

Even if we are without such obligations, as most of us eventually will be, the ritual of Hallowing assumes a spirituality where we care for ourselves. We must not deny this or put it off, although some of us are prone to do just that well into our fifties and sixties, caring minimally for ourselves only because it enables us to tend to others. That, however, is not the hallowing impulse, which assumes our essential worth, our essential dignity, and our essential right to care.

In older adult life, such care begins when we hear the summons to the Sabbath of Jubilee and say our initial, mature no. It develops as we set aside time for stillness and receptivity. It leads us into thick listening and prayerful awareness. And it does all these through turning us to the Care at the earth's heart, the Wise Caregiver who cared us into life and does not let us go.

That Caregiver is the Care at the core of this ritual. It is the Care found in our love for the planet, each other, and ourselves. The Divine Mystery is the caring in Care itself, the promise and guarantee that the universe is not destined for destruction. The Care who walked along the river bank is finally revealed to be one with the Care Who is Creator and Sacred One, beckoning us to hallow a Sabbath of complete rest.

Three

*P*ROCLAIMING *F*REEDOM

Proclaim liberty throughout the land to all its inhabitants.
Lev. 25:10

Over the years, I've discovered one poem echoes the dreams of Jubilee women more than any other: Jenny Joseph's "Warning." She follows her initial declaration, "When I am an old woman, I shall wear purple,/With a red hat which doesn't go, and doesn't suit me." with a provocative list of other plans that resonate in the souls of those of us over 50.

> And I shall spend my pension on brandy and summer gloves
> And satin sandals, and say we've no money for butter.
> I shall sit down on the pavement when I'm tired
> And gobble up samples in shops and press alarm bells
> And run my stick along the public railings
> And make up for the sobriety of my youth.

Then she gathers momentum and becomes more daring.

I shall go out in my slippers in the rain
And pick the flowers in other people's gardens
And learn to spit.

She makes comparisons:

You can wear terrible shirts and grow more fat
And eat three pounds of sausages at a go
Or only bread and pickle for a week
And hoard pens and pencils and beermats and things in
    boxes.
But now we must have clothes that keep us dry
And pay our rent and not swear in the street
And set a good example for the children.
We must have friends to dinner and read the papers.

Finally, she proposes a way out.

But maybe I ought to practise a little now?
So people who know me are not too shocked and
    surprised
When suddenly I am old, and start to wear purple.

Whenever I recite Joseph's poem with a group of Jubilee
women, they signal the shock of recognition the words send
through them. They laugh; they applaud. They appreciate the
poet speaking their dreams, saying with magnificent wit,
"When I am an old woman, I shall be free." Through their responses they affirm, "Yes, she's right. Becoming old women
means becoming free. It means claiming liberty as our
birthright."

Proclaiming Freedom is Jubilee Time's third ritual. Having entered the land the Divine Mystery has given us and paused to nourish hallowing through Sabbath listening, awareness, and care, we now proclaim liberty throughout the land to all its inhabitants—including ourselves, our children, and our grandchildren.

The twenty-fifth chapter of Leviticus offered a wealth of detail to early biblical-era people on how to proclaim liberty. They were to let go of property, returning it to its original owner in the fiftieth year. They were to release the land from its obligation to produce. They were to cancel outstanding debts. "The land shall not be sold in perpetuity," said their God, "for the land is mine."

The fiftieth year became a year for general amnesty. Employers were to release not only property but people, including those who didn't have money to buy redemption.

> If any who are dependent on you become so impoverished they sell themselves to you, you shall not make them serve as slaves. They shall remain with you as hired or bound laborers. They shall serve with you until the year of the jubilee. Then, they and their children with them shall be free from your authority; they shall go back to their own family and return to their ancestral property. (Lev. 25:39–41)

Such declarations of release were common thousands of years ago. Secular documents from the era clearly show Akkadian and Neo-Assyrian kings and rulers, neighbors of the early Israelites, regularly extending general amnesties to prisoners, debtors, and enslaved people. But the Hebrews' proclamation

of liberty differed from those of their secular counterparts because it came from the Holy One, not from human beings—
whether they were kings or not. Freedom came *through* the
Israelites who acted as God's agents, not *from* them, because it
wasn't theirs to give. It was political freedom, yes, but even
more, it was spiritual and moral freedom, a gift flowing from
the Divine Mystery who is the real Sovereign of the people
and the Creator of human freedom. The command to "proclaim liberty to *all* the earth's inhabitants" implicitly teaches

EXERCISE 1

Tallying Our Freedoms

Begin this exercise by attending to your breath and inhal-
ing/exhaling on the word *freedom* for five minutes. When
you feel quiet and centered, respond slowly and thought-
fully to the following questions. Record your responses in
your journal. If you're in a group, discuss with one another
how you felt doing the exercise, and share any responses
you feel comfortable talking about.

1. Recall an experience in your life when you canceled a
   debt someone owed you. How did doing that make
   you feel?
2. Recall an experience in your life when someone canceled
   a debt you owed. How did their doing that make you feel?

that no one is completely free until everyone else knows release from bondage. (See Exercise 1.)

PROCLAIMING LIBERTY IN JUBILEE TIME

In this chapter, we consider what the proclamation of liberty means for us. For one thing, we'll see it takes a long time to become free: often half a lifetime. For another, we'll find that

3. Do you possess any "property" that you need to let go? If so, what is it, and what keeps you from releasing it?

4. Is there property in your life you're waiting to have returned to you? How might you bring the waiting to a resolution?

5. From the same root as *amnesia*, the word *amnesty* originally meant "forgetfulness" or "intentional overlooking." Is there anything in your life for which you'd love to be granted amnesty? Something you'd like forgotten or overlooked? By whom? How do you think the amnesty would make you feel?

6. Have you ever granted amnesty to anyone? If so, what was the person's reaction? What was yours?

7. Is there anyone in your life toward whom you owe release—either an individual or a group of people?

8. What, so far, has been the greatest release of your life?

an essential element in Jubilee liberation is the freeing of age itself. As we cross the Jubilee threshold and listen thickly to life's second half, we'll realize it's imperative for Jubilarians to liberate the concept of age from condescending, discriminatory stereotypes in order to claim our personal identity as mature moral players.

And finally, we'll discover that to proclaim freedom is more than a private and personal statement. Like the contemporary women's liberation movement so closely linked to it, Jubilee liberation is relational. It's a social, communal spirituality linking us to others and to two groups in particular. One is made up of people less fortunate than ourselves. The other is made up of our daughters and granddaughters. Jubilee proclaims liberation not only for adults; "their children with them [also] shall be free" (Lev. 25:41).

A LONG TIME COMING

In the Bible, as in all human life, liberation and freedom are ideals: hard-sought and hard-earned. Biblical teaching helps us transform these ideals into reality by asking us to observe ritual practices at specific intervals to keep freedom's importance alive. The weekly Sabbath teaches that other people aren't for our use; the seventh-year Sabbath teaches us to free the land; the fifty-year Sabbath of Sabbaths marks a general amnesty. Yet even with such reminders, many of us resist freedom, even conspire with forces that hamper its taking root within us.

I've met such resistance regularly in groups of women; I suspect we all have. Sometimes, the sign is reluctance to acknowledge women's lack of freedom in today's world: "We don't really have it so bad." I recognize this resistance in my own history. I easily—and sheepishly—recall my reactions as the modern women's movement caught fire more than twenty-five years ago. Listening to calls for liberation, I remember thinking they really didn't apply to me: I'd been to college; I was finishing a doctorate at an Ivy League university; I was in the nine percent of graduate-school professors who were women. It took me several years, first denying barriers to my freedom, then gradually naming patterns of repression, to recognize that none of the economic, political, social, or religious rules were fair when it came to women—including me.

Institutional doors are beginning to open to us, especially in the United States, where equality under law continues to receive more and more guarantees. Still, the situation could stand a lot of improvement. In the United States, women earn between seventy and eighty percent of what men do; the glass ceiling curtails women's movement to upper-level positions in academia, law, and medicine (as the stained-glass ceiling does in religion); and government estimates report more than one million attacks on women by their husbands and companions yearly, indicating that many men still think they have a right to batter women. In a number of countries abroad, women's human rights are either abused or nonexistent. In Morocco, for example, the law excuses a man who kills his wife if she is caught in the act of adultery, although a woman would not be excused for killing her husband in the same circumstance. In India, dowry deaths—a phenomenon in which a groom or his family kills his wife out of anger because her dowry is insufficient—continue to be a serious problem.

These broader patterns of bondage, established over forty thousand years of human history, end slowly. But so do internal, personal self-bindings. Some restrictions can be a comfort: the responsibilities that limit us, such as children, hard work, and caring for lonely parents, are often the sources of our emotional sustenance as well. We may also deliberately set up our own restrictions and limits and allow them to confine and control us. For example, we may use our age as an excuse to avoid starting law school after 50, even though we have the prerequisites, pleading, "I'm really too old." Or we may refuse a new and exciting job offer—at better pay—because it asks us to use capacities we've allowed to get rusty. For many of us, freedom is frightening.

Fear of freedom must be worked through in a caring community or even in long-term therapy. Like Jubilee itself, it can take over fifty years to confront and repair this deep-seated resistance. After I'd made this point during a recent Jubilee retreat, a participant came up to me. "I just want to affirm one thing you said that's been terribly true for me," she confided. Referring to her recovery from a painful personal restriction that had limited her for decades, she concurred, "It really *did* take fifty years!"

In other conversations, I've met women who identify the restrictions in their lives as burdens. Mandy, celebrating sobriety at 62, reported, "Besides fogging up my head and draining my energy, my drinking was a terrible burden. I looked at myself in the mirror one morning and said, 'You're 52 years old. Why are you carrying this dead weight?' " Then she added, smiling, "I began going to AA regularly and I've been sober for ten years. The burden's so much less, and that's made me feel free."

Listening to her, 65-year-old Joan said, "I know it's not as serious a problem as your battle with alcohol, but I remember feeling burdened when I looked in my closet." Retired from her job as a coordinator of volunteers in a million-member nonprofit organization, she said, "I realized I'd never wear those five-hundred-dollar suits again. Why was I holding on to them?" Sensing an "inner drag," in which the burden wasn't so much the clothes as the fashion bondage they symbolized, she called her 27-year-old niece, a neophyte stock analyst who couldn't afford such a wardrobe. "Ellie," she told her, "I've got to clean my closets. How about taking these suits off my hands, and having them retailored to fit you?"

Barb, a pediatric nurse about to celebrate her fiftieth birthday, put it this way. "When I was younger, I thought real life had to be serious." Life got freer for her, she reports, "as I learned to laugh and lighten up; to set more realistic priorities with more realistic expectations."

Also about to celebrate her fiftieth birthday, Laura made a comparison too. "I miss having the vigor and enthusiasm I see in my daughters, 24 and 22," she writes, "but I wouldn't want to be involved in the 'game playing' they're enduring in choosing a career, a lifestyle, friends, lovers." Characterizing those games as restrictions, she compares them with her own life, where she's at another point, "better able to enjoy the present moment than I was when I was younger and wouldn't allow myself to take time. Now I'm free to take all the time I want."

To unburden ourselves and successfully complete the long trek to freedom, we've got to harness our psychic energy. In earlier years, we've often put that energy into what Laura identifies as life games—making it on the job or choosing and cultivating friends and lovers—that often result in putting parts of ourselves on hold.

But now, as we journey through life's second half, the proclamation of freedom calls us to act and express ourselves as

EXERCISE 2

The Flight from Freedom

After attending to your breath and inhaling/exhaling regularly on the word *freedom,* pause to consider the presence of a reality in your life that you consider an obstruction inhibiting your freedom.

1. What burden do you carry that keeps you from being free?
2. How long have you carried it?
3. How long have you realized it's holding you down?
4. Try to list three to five ways this burden limits you.
5. Now list three to five of your personal gifts—qualities or energies—that could help you release it.
6. Choose one action you will take in the coming week as an initial letting-go. Subsequently, as you repeat this exercise, choose additional actions that will continue to release you from this burden.
7. Conclude by calling on the Freedom at the core of the universe to accompany you in this action of liberation.

we choose, urging us to rewrite the rules of the game to our own specifications. Although we are now more self-reliant and less concerned about being who others expect us to be, we also recognize that these earlier expectations served as painful although not entirely useless preparation for the release into freedom. They provided what 50-year-old Lynne refers to as "the experiences that have brought us to where we are now." (See Exercise 2.)

THE LIBERATION—
AND THE LIBERATING—OF AGE

When we claim our freedom and enter the terrain of age, seeking to learn how to proclaim liberty throughout this land to all its inhabitants, a fresh realization grips us. We are confronting an unknown land, a *terra incognita*. We're exploring it, even creating it, as we go along. We have only the sketchiest of maps.

At the turn of the twentieth century, women's life expectancy was 46. The nuances and the fullness of life past 50 weren't major concerns. Only in the years of our own elderhood has life expectancy changed for women, now hovering close to 80 in the United States. Gail Sheehy admits that as late as 1976, when she wrote her influential book *Passages,* she rarely touched on life beyond 50. Not only couldn't she imagine herself this old, but most people she interviewed thought of 50 as over the hill.

But even as attention has turned toward the second half of life, more specifically to the years between fifty and one hundred, certain assumptions about age have precluded our asking the right questions. Until now, inquiry into later life has focused on the five percent of the over-65 population in nursing homes or the five percent of the aging suffering from Alzheimer's, not on ordinary older people. Inquiry has focused not on age in itself, but on age in relation to youth. In fact, the defining characteristic of age has become *no longer being young*. Youth provides our lens, our angle of vision. A (if not *the*) guiding question in age has turned out to be, "What does it mean—physically, sexually, psychologically—to leave youth behind?"

For far too long, we elders have been and done what too many students of aging, developmental theorists, or even gerontologists have told us to be and do. We've been taught that age is equivalent to dealing with sickness, loneliness, impairment, and decline, and we've bought into the presumption that these conditions constitute the meaning of age. Even as I began writing this book, part of me was surprised to read responses to my questionnaire revealing vital, involved older women who failed to focus on decline and impairment. I wondered whether they were unusual, and concluded they weren't.

In realizing that, I've discovered something I now want to proclaim. From the rooftop of my soul I want to shout, "We've been asking the wrong questions about age!" The central questions most fitting for us aren't how to deal with pathologies or inevitable decline and death, although the last two are relevant because the way of all living things is to decline and die. But that's not the meaning of age. Age's central questions are more along the lines of those in Exercise 3.

Each woman's answers to these questions will differ to some degree. Following are four of my own responses to question 1.

EXERCISE 3

Probing a New Set of Questions

Before we explore some more general responses to new questions about age, pause to listen to your own responses. Begin by attending to your breathing, becoming centered and quiet, perhaps using the mantra "Listen, listen, listen to your heart" for an initial period of three minutes. Then listen to your heart's probing, and respond to the following questions:

1. Now that you have entered the land of aging, what freedoms await you?
2. What are some resistances to age once binding you that are now gone?
3. Complete: For me, the best thing about being free to grow old is _____.

Share your responses with one other person, or write them in your journal, before considering those that follow.

We are free to cherish age. That's a mighty course change in an ageist society, so obsessed with youth it's difficult to find the faces of over-50 (and certainly over-60) women in advertising or playing romantic leads against agemates such as Sean Connery or Robert Redford. For those female leads, Hollywood wants women in their thirties—Michelle Pfeiffer or Demi Moore—saying of still-gorgeous women in their forties, fifties, or beyond, "We can't use her. She's over the hill."

But as we bid youth a gentle farewell and embrace the freedoms of age, we know we're not over some hill, but in a lush, green valley, full of fresh growth. So we ask, "What does Hollywood know about it?" and turn to age as a source of truth—and strength and power—in our lives, one to be embraced, not feared. We discover that cherishing and befriending age feels right, fits, the way flats do after decades of high heels.

One simple way to cherish our age is to stop creating false images of ourselves by trying to look younger than we are, to abandon "age passing" in favor of proudly exhibiting our actual years. Some of us may add back the years we knocked off our age when we turned 50; others may forego makeup. At 58, I stopped coloring my hair, and began greeting the now silver-haired me when I looked in the mirror. When I did, my eyes revealed an older woman at peace with herself and in tune with her inner elder.

Embracing honesty regarding our physical selves allows us to pierce the surface and reach our deeper spiritual selves. Releasing superficial obsessions that may constrict us, we become alert to interior capacities ripe for development, including personal power, honest sexuality, and deep contemplation. The fullness of years that Jubilee celebrates becomes the basis for a genuinely new spirituality that liberates us even further, into wisdom.

We are free to be wise. Sometimes, when I end a workshop, I go around the room and ask women to answer the question,

"Who are you becoming?" Last week, when I did that, Alla, in her late fifties, answered, "I'm becoming a wise woman," reminding all of us present that that could be true for us too.

Becoming wise, like becoming free, takes a long time. Wisdom is a kind of knowledge based on intuition, but the intuition, in turn, comes from living and being in touch with the range of experience long life offers. It's cumulative. But it's physical too, centered in the body and in blood, birth, and pain. It involves acting on hunches, especially the hunch that sometimes the risky action is the right one, the desperate move the only possibility.

Genuine wisdom involves learning from the wisdoms of other forgotten or overlooked people, out of a humility that knows none of us has all the answers. It means learning from blind women how to trust our own fingertips; from women who use wheelchairs how to travel the up ramp; from women of color how to challenge systems that chain us.

But wisdom also involves admitting that we can make terrible mistakes, have huge gaps in our understanding, and always retain the capacity for evil. Whenever I read the entire twenty-fifth chapter of Leviticus, I'm reminded of this. For despite the extraordinary wisdom of Jubilee, there's a dreadful fault line crossing it: the passage that allows *some* slaves to remain in bondage, as long as they aren't "our" people.

> As for the male and female slaves whom you may have, it is from the nations around you that you may acquire male and female slaves. You may also acquire them from among the aliens residing with you, and from their families that are with you, who have been born in your land and they may be your property. You may

keep them as a possession for your children after you,
for them to inherit as property. These you may treat as
slaves, but as for your fellow Israelites, no one shall rule
over the other with harshness. (Lev. 25:44–46)

I used to be terribly shocked by that, wondering how the first
Jubilee people could be so unseeing. I thought of these lines as
a scar, a fissure of evil, flawing the wholeness of Jubilee. I still
do. But I also suspect that this passage, repudiated in modern
times so that the teaching and practice of Jubilee today does
extend to enslaved persons, was left there to remind me of terrible omissions in my own life, places of evil I am capable of
ignoring.

We are free to let go. A central and recurring theme in Western mystical tradition is detachment, which speaks to the
promise of letting go, release, and redemption. Although some
interpret it as cool distancing from a situation or self-absorbed
withdrawal from working toward justice, it is actually a facet of
liberation.

Complementing this tradition, the *Bhagavad Gita* of Hinduism teaches that the detached person is active, but that being
active differs here from its usual meaning. A person now acts
without looking for the fruits of her actions. Whatever we are
called to do or are able to do is now done for its own sake, not
for the sake of results or rewards. And although such an attitude doesn't necessarily depend on age, it characterizes later
years more than it does youth.

Expressing her own growing detachment, 50-year-old
Anna Mae, who describes herself as "a youngster beginning
old age," writes that as she ages, she experiences the power of
"a growing freedom and urgency to say what I care about

bilee woman must be earned by doing things that contribute to the freedom of others, things as simple as praying for their freedom and as complicated as joining the Peace Corps, the way Lillian Carter did at 68. Such activity is a sign the Spirit is upon me also.

The breadth of Jubilee liberty is reiterated in the New Testament in the gospel of Luke. When Jesus returns to Nazareth, where he was raised ("Each of you shall return to your place and to your people, where you were brought up"), and goes to the synagogue to speak to his neighbors, he asks for the scroll containing the Book of Isaiah and reads the passage quoted above. Then he adds, referring to Jubilee's relevance to the people gathered in the synagogue, "Today, this scripture is fulfilled in your hearing." The promise of Jubilee cannot be fulfilled in isolation, but only as part of a community.

This meaning of Jubilee as the proclamation of liberty beyond ourselves is alive in modern times. In 1991, for example, missionaries from Panama asked the United States and the World Bank to declare a year of Jubilee in 1992, the five hundredth anniversary of the voyages of Columbus. But they didn't ask it for themselves. They requested it instead for Central America's poor African-American and indigenous peoples, overburdened by crushing and exorbitant debts and referred to globally, as if it were their only identity, as debtor nations. The missionaries saw the relevance of release, forgiveness, and amnesty both beyond themselves and beyond biblical times.

In the United States, the proclamation of liberation from bondage compels us to consider our prisons. We are remarkably ignorant of women's prisons, for example, and the toll prison takes on mothers and children. Unlike in the Bible, where prisoners are not criminals or convicts but prisoners of war, captives, hostages, or victims of government oppression, our prisons are too often places of warehousing for many non-violent offenders who have broken civil laws and who might be better sentenced to community service. Prisons neither re-habilitate nor offer new beginnings.

"Lila served two years for lying about a $167 welfare check. She was offered one year if she would plea-bargain, but she refused, went to trial, and got two years," wrote one aging woman prisoner, reporting on this system. "Lila still insists she never cashed that check," the reporter continues. " 'I think it was my cousin done it, but I didn't get that money.' " Even worse, when her sentence is finished Lila will still know noth-ing of budgeting her welfare check, will still not know how to read and write.

The Jubilee woman who tells Lila's story was also an in-mate. Jean Harris was finally released in 1993 after serving thirteen years, and is now in her seventies. A graduate of both Smith College and New York's Bedford Hills Correctional Fa-cility for Women, she wryly shares Lila's plight with the rest of us, pointing out that we all know people who take $167 tax deductions at lunch, and asking whether as taxpayers we have more reason to pay for those lunches than for Lila's check, or Lila's future. In her own Jubilee Time, Jean Harris is devoting herself to women's prison reform, and to mothers in prison and their children, modeling the kind of complete Jubilee spir-ituality to which all of us are called.

The women responding to me described many ways they addressed the relational element in this ritual of Jubilee spirituality. Cathy, a 50-year-old Hispanic-American from Albuquerque who is an educational administrator, said, "I engage in advocacy in several areas, especially in family

---

EXERCISE 4

The following ceremony embodies the relational character of proclaiming freedom beyond ourselves.

A cup is passed around a circle of people gathered together for prayer and communion or for the sharing of a meal. Before each person drinks from the cup, she removes two or three drops. As she removes them she says, "I remove these drops in remembrance of the poor of our world, and in solidarity with them. We cannot drink the cup in all its fullness until there is enough for everyone."

---

crises, which helps me keep in touch with dispossessed and oppressed people." Joanna, a 56-year-old registered nurse, told me, "I *need* to be in service to the community in some way," and described doing volunteer work both for a hospice and for Meals on Wheels.

Some women drew connections between their own and others' liberation. Shirley, a 57-year-old Chinese-American from Phoenix, also a nurse, wrote, "The more involved I am, the more interested in life I am. The more interested, the more learning takes place in me. The more 'smarts' I get, the more I need to participate. So it isn't unusual for me to be in demonstrations for refugees, for farm workers, at vigils against capital punishment, at political rallies, or speaking for women's rights in the church and in the marketplace." Shirley also performs community work with Central American refugees, and with homeless, hungry, and disenfranchised women and men.

The range of people and issues calling for liberation is as broad as the earth itself. Still, one group has a particular claim on us: our daughters and granddaughters. We owe them; as their mothers and grandmothers, we have a responsibility to remove from their shoulders whatever burdens we can. Aware of this, Jubilee women routinely say, "I've been given a great deal in my life. Now it's my turn to give back." That profoundly spiritual impulse—to release, to return what belongs to others, to find

EXERCISE 5

Choosing a Daughter

For this exercise, choose a young woman to accompany you mentally through the last section of this chapter. If you're a mother of daughters, or have granddaughters, choose one of them; if you're not, choose a girl or young woman as a surrogate daughter/granddaughter.

You may want to do this exercise twice: once with the girl or young woman you have chosen, but first with your younger self.

1. For what about this young woman are you most grateful?
2. What gifts and talents has she already discovered in herself?

out what belongs to whom and give it back—reflects this Jubilee ritual. For if not you, who? And if not now, when?

PROCLAIMING LIBERTY
TO THE NEXT GENERATION

We who are Jubilarians are the first generation of women to enter our mature years after the modern women's movement. We have its wisdom to offer not only to our contemporaries,

3. What gifts and talents do you see in her that she hasn't yet learned to honor?
4. What's your greatest concern or fear for her?
5. What about your relationship do you cherish?
6. What about your relationship do you mourn?
7. Is there anything you've asked her to carry for you that you realize limits her freedom? Something you've placed on her as a burden? Have you ever talked about this with her? Might you?
8. Are you aware of burdens *society* places on her? If so, name them. Are you aware of burdens she places on herself?
9. Is there anything she's asked you to carry that you need to release back to her?
10. Conclude with a prayerful expression of gratitude for the life of this younger woman or girl.

but to the generations coming after us. That wisdom can change their futures, and we can offer it by affirming their freedom to speak with their own voices and to create their own spirituality. (See Exercise 5.)

VOICE

Many older women describe Jubilee Time as a period when they reclaim their voices and become free to speak. "Growing older, I find it easier to express my feelings," says Mary, 63. "The best thing about growing older is I'm not afraid to speak my mind," responds Maureen at 50. "I can assert what I know or hope or believe with more confidence now that I'm older," reports Berta at 65.

As Jubilarians, they are reflecting upon a time earlier in life when they monitored the speaking of their actual thoughts or kept expression of their feelings in check. As many Jubilee women I've met agree, this didn't necessarily mean they stopped talking. As women, they'd learned that one of the most powerful ways to mask what they really thought was to talk a great deal, earning reputations as gabbers. In their sometimes incessant talking, however, they no longer risked articulating what they really knew, evoking for me a memory of poet Muriel Rukeyser's question: "What would happen if one woman told the truth about her life?" and her powerful answer, "The world would split open."

These comments dovetail with experiences being reported today about the generations of women who are following us. Extensive research—by the American Association of University Women, by the Canadian Federation of Teachers, by Carol

Gilligan and her associates at Harvard—has shown that girls start limiting both expression of feeling and assertion of what they know, hope, and believe as early as age 11, a habit that can last well into adult life. Researchers refer to this too-frequent occurrence as a "developmental loss" and pinpoint it as a loss of voice.

Early in life, they report, at 6, 7, and 8, girls assume conflict and disagreement are natural in human relations and speak up without hesitating if they're hurt or don't want to go along with their elders or peers. It doesn't occur to them to hide their feelings. Like the heroine of *Rebecca of Sunnybrook Farm*, they're "plucky at two" and "dauntless at five." But they begin to hedge this pluckiness, openness, and honesty as they come to the end of childhood.

Somewhere around the age of 11, too many of them start to mute their voices, to silence themselves. Although they might at first glance be considered talkative, like their mothers and grandmothers, they *don't* talk about what concerns them most, especially human interactions. At this age they face a dilemma. Their first option is to continue being open and as- sertive and direct, speaking out when they disagree. But when they do that, they're labeled "bossy" or "a loudmouth" and get placed on the margins socially.

Their other option is to stop saying what they believe and know in their hearts. They erase their voices; they lock them away. They become alienated from themselves, marginalized in a different way, distanced from who they really are. As one 11- year-old put it, "When I do that, I can tell it's not really me."

If such loss of voice happens, it begins around 11 or 12 and continues to a frightening degree in the following years, lasting well into adulthood for too many women. It is even

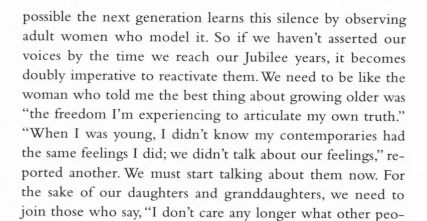

EXERCISE 6

The Return of Voice

In this exercise, we reflect on the movement from silence to speech in order to understand how and when at least some women's voices are silenced, and how and when these same women reclaim their voices. Ideally, this is a group exercise, but you can prepare for it personally by answering the following.

1. Recall an experience in your adult life when you chose not to speak although you wanted to and had something to say.
2. What circumstances or conditions held you back?
3. Who else was present?

possible the next generation learns this silence by observing adult women who model it. So if we haven't asserted our voices by the time we reach our Jubilee years, it becomes doubly imperative to reactivate them. We need to be like the woman who told me the best thing about growing older was "the freedom I'm experiencing to articulate my own truth." "When I was young, I didn't know my contemporaries had the same feelings I did; we didn't talk about our feelings," reported another. We must start talking about them now. For the sake of our daughters and granddaughters, we need to join those who say, "I don't care any longer what other peo-

4. How did you feel afterward?
5. Now recall an experience when you chose to speak.
6. What were the circumstances or conditions this time? How did they differ from those you identified in response to question 2?
7. Who else was present?
8. What influence did your age have on your speaking or not speaking?
9. If you could give one piece of advice to a silent or silenced woman or girl about claiming her voice, what would it be? Be as specific as possible.
10. When you convene in a group to share your responses, create a set of instructions on voice, drawn from the responses to question 9. Share them with the girl you brought to the preceding exercise.

ple think of me," and emulate 57-year-old Annie, who asserts, "I can be myself whether I'm accepted or not." (See Exercise 6.)

While discussing this issue in a workshop, a woman told the rest of us that she had suddenly recognized how often she and her daughter say to her 5-year-old granddaughter, "Jennie, stop talking." "Jennie, keep still." "Jennie, be a lady." Our conversation made her want to rush home and "proclaim liberty throughout the land," especially to the inhabitant named Jennie. "I've got to change my advice to her," she said. "She's got to *keep* talking. She's got to hold on to her voice."

Spirituality and the Next Generations

If spirituality is our way of being in the world in the light of the Mystery at the core of the universe, it incorporates our particular way of being in the world *as women*. Only in the last few decades have we begun to develop a genuine human spirituality, one that places the female voice, girlhood, and womanhood at its center in community with men and boys. Only in the last few decades have we realized almost all our religious systems and religious language have come from men in positions of power. We need to be liberated from constricting metaphors such as singing of ourselves as soldiers marching onward, or of God as a "mighty fortress." With Hildegard of Bingen, who lived centuries ago, we need to reclaim a divinity who is "the breeze that nurtures all things," "the rain coming from the dew causing the grass to laugh with the joy of life," "the aroma of holy work."

We also need to remember that belonging to a temple, church, or mosque is only one way of living out a spirituality; belonging to a religious institution isn't necessarily the same thing as being a religious person. Nonetheless, for the next generation of women, the daughters and granddaughters born from our bodies or our spirits, the presence or absence of women in the central ritual roles of any communion, any society, has enormous consequences. Although I'm not an Episcopalian, I've participated in many Episcopal liturgies. When Betty McWhorter or Carter Heyward presides, I can testify to the liberation I experience when such a priest extends her hands in blessing or holds bread and cup in those hands and says to the gathered community, "This is my Body. This is my Blood." She's not "other" to me in the way a man is. Instead, she stands in for me; she's *like* me.

A priest is a mediator; as older women, all of us are mediators and priests for those coming after us, transmitting to them a spirituality richer and fuller than the one we received. We owe the exercise of such priesthood to the next generation so they are not bound, as too many of us were, by the idea that God is male and that they are inherently flawed because they are female. We can practice this priesthood by bringing our daughters and granddaughters—and sons and grandsons—to the religious rituals that mean the most to us, especially when a woman presides, seeking out such settings and such women for the sake of the children.

Furthermore, we can alert our children to places where alone, or alongside men, women tell the story, or break the bread, or share the cup, or repeat the prophetic words that name our responsibilities to the world. As participants in such ceremonies, the next generation can learn with Isaiah and Jesus that the Spirit of God is upon them also. In every city of the land, circles of such women and men exist, and any sensitive local rabbi, minister, priest, or spiritual leader can direct us to them. Sitting in such circles, we can teach our daughters and granddaughters rituals naming their foremothers with chants like "I'm the daughter of Aisha and Hagar, of Rebecca and Leah, of Mary and Teresa." Especially when those circles represent women across religious lines, they can become opportunities for Muslims, Jews, and Christians to name ancestors in a common experience that can liberate them from ancient divisions and separations.

And finally, we can proclaim to our daughters and granddaughters the power in talking about and praying to the Sacred Mystery as She, Her, Mother, Goddess, and Holy Crone by talking and praying this way ourselves. Playwright Ntozake

Shange's poetic revelation, "I found god in myself and I loved her; I loved her fiercely," has come terribly late into our lives, but it need not be so for them. Today, we who are grand-mothers and women elders can pass down a tradition pro-claiming such a female divinity, so that they too may learn to love Her fiercely and in doing so find liberty. In Her com-pany, we and our children with us can then turn together to Jubilee's next ritual, and make the journey back to our place and to our people.

Four

*T*HE *J*UBILEE *J*OURNEYS

You shall return, every one of you, to your property and every one of you to your family.

Lev. 25:10

I once heard a story describing a striking incident in a women's studies course. The students were members of a general education program, older than typical undergraduates. One evening, most of them hadn't been able to do the assigned reading. So on the spot the teachers asked them to pair off and tell each other the story of their mothers' lives.

The energy was fantastic, yet when they reconvened, many reported discovering they didn't really know their mothers' stories or knew only parts of them. That led to further conversations with their mothers outside of class.

A woman of Greek descent found that at 17 her mother had walked out of her inland village and made her way to Athens. When she got there, she embarrassed her city relatives by earning her own money for passage to the United States, rather than remain and continue to endure an uncle's sexual advances. Accounts like this provoked class members to probe their ancestry and roots further. They had hit upon a way to make return journeys to their places of origin and to encounter the people from whom they'd come.

Such journeys are the heart of this ritual. Having crossed the threshold into Jubilee Time, paused for hallowing, and proclaimed liberty throughout the land to all its inhabitants, we now explore how that liberty impels us to go back to our

---

EXERCISE 1

Telling a Life

This is an exercise to work on not only here but throughout this ritual. In it, you will tell two lives—your mother's and your father's—sympathetically, from their viewpoints, as far as you are able. If your parents are still living, you may want to interview them, taping your interview or recording it in writing.

Begin by responding to the following questions, taking no more than an hour at any given time with each parent individually, or with both at the same time. If your parents are no longer living, you may want to use your imagination, letting your parents speak in their own voices ("I am Alice, born in . . ."; "I am Bert, born in . . ."). You may frame the questions in the form of a letter to them, and invite them to respond on their own. If you don't know the answers, you may decide to contact other family members who do.

own places and people. The command to do so is repeated three times in the twenty-fifth chapter of Leviticus, reinforcing how seriously we must take it: "It shall be a jubilee for you; you shall return, every one of you, to your property and every one of you to your family," reads verse 10. "In this year of jubilee, you shall return, every one of you, to your property," repeats verse 13. And then, speaking about bound laborers, it resounds once more in verse 41: "[Not only you, but]

1. What is your mother's full name?
2. How did she get these names?
3. Describe her childhood years, passions, and ambitions. Do the same for her teenage and young adult years, passions, and ambitions.
4. Describe the place(s) where she grew up.
5. Describe her adult life up to 50. What were some of its major incidents?
6. Describe her adult life after 50. What was Jubilee Time like for her?
7. What have been her greatest joys? Greatest sorrows?
8. How are you most like and most unlike her?
9. Giving yourself lots of silence in order to hear the answer, what are some things your mother wants to say to you now that you are a Jubilee woman?
10. What do you want to say to her?

Repeat the exercise, telling your father's life.

they and their children with them shall be free from your authority; they shall go back to their own family, and return to their ancestral property."

Now it is our turn. Like those laborers and indentured servants released from their bonds, we are now liberated to make our own ancestral journey.

We can fashion it in several ways. Armed with maps and guidebooks and airline tickets, we can travel on a *physical* journey, a pilgrimage back to our family's place of origin, and fulfill the Jubilee command to the letter. Assisted by memory, we can make a *daughter's* journey, with plans to honor our parents' lives, commemorate their joys and their sorrows, and mend any damaged connections between us. We can make an imaginative *mythical* journey down to archetypal figures who are foremothers in a sense other than family. And we can incorporate each of these into the journey *toward age and death,* as memory, mourning, and myth guide us on the ultimate path home.

Before we turn to each of these, however, we must situate ourselves as women with a heritage. To give us a context, even though we may resist, be fearful, or uncover terrible gaps in our knowledge, we start with a process that is fundamental to this journey: telling our mothers' and our fathers' lives. (See Exercise 1.)

THE OUTWARD JOURNEY

The outward journey is to actual places of origin, birth, or ancestry, sometimes in our own land, often in other countries.

Some of us make these journeys in the flesh. I made the first of mine in 1969, traveling to Ireland with my mother. At the time she was 70, and although she'd visited her father's farm, she'd never seen her mother's birthplace. An aged cousin brought us to the place my grandmother had lived until, at 16, she emigrated to New York. That day I learned that my grandmother, whom I'd never met—she died when my mother was 11—had spent her girlhood in a cave cut into the soft side of a hill. We walked inside, our feet touching the same earth floor hers had, our sight adjusting to the windowless space. She'd lived a life of poverty I could barely imagine. That day I received her life in that cave as part of my heritage; my mother received it as part of hers.

Several years later, I went back. Bulldozers and developers had arrived and the cave was gone. I had almost missed the experience of finding my grandmother's place, and with it, the knowledge of an essential part of my ancestry.

Mary Ann made an outward journey too. Two years ago, at 50, she traveled from New Jersey to southwest Texas to see the place in which her father had lived and died. She still remembered happy occasions, regular outings with this man who had become lost to her when she was 11. ("Don't call him 'the man who left us,' " she told me. "That's not how I think of him. Call him 'the man I once knew; the man I was close to; the man lost to me.' ") Now, decades later, she suddenly needed this pilgrimage. She had to recover his life because it was part of her own.

In Texas, she talked with people who'd known him and discovered her father had been loved in the community and had contributed significantly to local political life. People's genuine reverence and appreciation for him touched her. But the interior, personal connections with her father that the journey made possible affected her more. She told me her journey had turned into "a way of being faithful."

EXERCISE 2

Roots

With paper and colored pens or crayons, draw your family tree. Create a symbol for the people you know and/or remember, or draw something (a color, a piece of clothing, an object) you associate with them. Draw an empty box next to those you never knew or don't remember.

How far back can you trace the women in your heritage? If you don't or can't identify them past two or three generations, list some possibilities that occur to you for tracing them. These include:

People who knew them
Agencies that might find them

"Faithful in what way?" I asked.

"I've always thought of my life as a journey to be faithful to who I am and what I'm supposed to be. Being faithful means accepting the circumstances that are *my* life. I had to make this journey because it let me live this fidelity." She paused for a moment. "It's allowed reconciliation too. I'm at a time when I'm closing the first half of my life, and I've got to do that in peace. My journey to Texas helped that happen." Then, conscious of the intersection of her journey with the beginning of her Jubilee years, she reflected, "As I think of it,

Birth records★
Marriage records
Death records
Immigration/citizenship records
Other records

Choose one woman whose story you don't know but want to pursue—your mother's grandmother; your father's sister; someone you resemble, like Catherine Noren's aunt (see page 94). Decide how you'll begin your detective work. If you have friends who'd like to do the same in their families, start a "Roots" group. Write down the first five steps you'll take in your search.

★Be prepared to discover, as one woman found in searching her Korean roots, that in some of the world's countries, "lineage books" record only the births of male children.

Jubilee could have destroyed me. But it didn't. Instead, it healed me where I needed healing.

"After the journey, I knew I had to continue the relationship with my dad," Mary Ann continued. "Even though he's dead—like my mother—I can still talk with him the way I do with her. But I needed his permission. I found myself saying, 'If you want to be part of my life now, you've got to give me a sign.' "

One night she got it. Keeping her apartment mate company watching a movie she really didn't want to see, she discovered the real reason she was staying up. Her breath stopped and her eyes filled as the main character spoke the movie's last lines. They were a father's words to children he barely knew: "You gotta excuse me," he said. "I don't know how to be a father because I've never been one. But if you want me to, I'll be one now."

Not everyone makes this outward journey through physical travel, as my mother and I did or as Mary Ann did. Photographer Catherine Hanf Noren tells of the day she found a pile of old photographs at her grandmother's house. The people in them were unfamiliar, although one young girl's face startled her because it mirrored her own. When she asked, her grandmother responded with a strong, mournful lament in which she introduced her granddaughter to aunts and uncles and cousins who'd perished in Hitler's Germany. The young woman with Catherine's features was an aunt she hadn't known existed.

That incident shaped her career and her destiny. Today Catherine is a professional photographer who, by preserving family images, enables Jew and non-Jew to participate in her journey, broadening the ritual return to roots beyond one woman's immediate experience.

When we become Jubilarians, the impulse to take part in an outward journey usually coincides with stirrings within us. Unlike adolescence and young adulthood, when we need distance from home and family in order to ask who we are, Jubilee Time prompts us to probe this question by exploring our roots, especially our parents' lives, so we can understand how they contributed to making us who we are. Some of this return journey occurs naturally, during the give-and-take of regular phone calls or brief visits. However, much of our search is an interior, contemplative expedition accomplished through meditation and memory. Whatever the form, and even though we are mothers and grand-

mothers ourselves, the journey is basically that of an adult daughter seeking to make her life complete. (See Exercise 2.)

THE DAUGHTER'S JOURNEY

By commanding a return to our place and our people, Jubilee
offers a ritual for honoring our parents. We often owe the best of
what we are to their being the best of what they are or were. We
may not have recognized their independent identities earlier in
life, mistakenly assuming that being our mother or our father was
their only role. We may not have noticed the range of human
qualities they possessed. As 65-year-old Natalie reported to me,
"One of the things I know now that I didn't when I was younger
is my mother's complexity; at this age I recognize and remember
all the ways she cherished us and battled for us and other people."

Birthdays, anniversaries, and funerals provide natural ritual
opportunities for such remembering. For Jim and Betty Ann's
fifty-fifth wedding anniversary, for example, each of their
brothers and sisters as well as their children wrote a letter to
them recalling incidents from their lives. Reading the letters
aloud to those who'd come to celebrate was a high point of
the anniversary party. During a recent Jubilee retreat, when I
asked people to reflect on possessions they cherished, Lois and
Janet both described receiving their grandmothers' journals as
birthday gifts. And when 52-year-old Georgia's uncle spoke at
his sister Eleanor's memorial service and described her childhood passion for taking in stray animals, Georgia told him, "I
never knew that about Mom."

At the same time, sore, tender places can exist in even the
finest relationships, especially the complicated one between

daughters and mothers. With age and freedom, we are ready to face these sore spots, and as we do, to understand what caused them.

The women's movement has fostered this work by instilling in us broader sensitivity to generational differences; research has illuminated how badly society can damage close female bonds, sometimes pitting one woman against another; and abundant resources exist today that are specifically designed to keep mothers and daughters connected. We grew up in another era, however, and sometimes lacked such supportive

---

EXERCISE 3

Affirming Gifts and Returning Burdens

Many of the gifts we receive from our mothers have positive effects in our lives and become part of us. We need to celebrate them. But there may be negative legacies we carry that we need to let go, because they don't belong to us. In this exercise we pause to reflect on both.

Begin by concentrating on your breath, quieting down and centering as you repeat the word *mother,* inhaling and exhaling on this word for at least ten breaths. Then answer the following questions.

1.   What positive gifts in your life come to you directly from your mother?

contexts in our early lives. So we may find, as Jubilarians, that still-painful parts of our relationships with our mothers need to be healed. The daughter's journey fosters such healing as we examine the burdens of daughterhood, the impulses to grieve, and ways to repair broken primary bonds.

THE BURDENS OF DAUGHTERHOOD

On the journey back to our place and people, some of us may carry a psychic burden because our relationship with our

2. Thank her for each of them, either in person, through a letter, or in an imagined conversation.
3. Is there any negative legacy you received or carried for her, particularly a grief or a sorrow that wasn't yours?
4. If there was and you still carry it, let it go. When and if it feels right, tell her about it in actual conversation or through a letter. If you can't do that, hold an imaginary conversation and write it down in your journal if that feels appropriate.
5. Resolve to send your mother flowers, or to plant them in her memory, to symbolize both your affirming gifts and your returning burdens.

Conclude the exercise with at least ten breaths on the word *mother.*

mother brought us sadness or pain. Perhaps we lost her to early death, or felt abandoned when she placed us in a foster home. Perhaps she suffered from chronic illness that regularly separated her from us, or endured clinical depression throughout her life, as 55-year-old Bobbie's mother has. Perhaps she was regularly drunk when we returned from school in the afternoon. Perhaps she really *did* dismiss us out of jealousy, dislike, or a complete inability to mother.

Perhaps none of these caused the burden. Instead we carry it because we are aware she was an unwanted daughter with untapped capacities. Perhaps she had a job in an era that had far fewer roles for women and far more reprisals for women who were "different," whether those differences stemmed from divorce, single parenthood, or a passion to succeed in a society that wanted them to stay home and keep still. We may carry a daughter's burden of guilt because we rejected our mother's values and style as dated or weak, and identified with our father's style and values instead. Intuitively, we knew we risked recapitulating our mother's life, and that possibility felt too dangerous, too close.

If we made these or similar choices as younger women, they return to haunt us in Jubilee Time, begging us to reconsider. Mothers of daughters ourselves, we now realize that difficulties in our relationship often came from impossible demands once made on women: by churches, by schools, and by the surrounding culture, especially in its advertising and its movies. The more aware of this we become, the more our mothers now appear to us as valiant but outmaneuvered fighters in a battle they were never meant to survive (as Audre Lorde put it), at least not as mothers. The journey back to our place and people reactivates a longing to be reconciled with them, a desire dormant or misunderstood until now. In Jubilee Time we can finally respond to it by naming our differences honestly, even as we learn to celebrate our mothers—as they are and were. (See Exercise 3.)

THE DAUGHTER'S GRIEF

Before psychologist and researcher Martha Robbins entered the second half of life, her mother died of cancer. As a way of coping with that loss and dealing with its ramifications for her own future, she designed a study based on a very specific question: how do midlife women respond to their mothers' deaths? In the course of that study she made two important discoveries with implications for Jubilee women.

One was that compared to the loss of a spouse or a child, the adult experience of a parent's death hasn't been considered significant in Western culture. Even though society still expects women to care for aging or ill parents, it also asks us to maintain an impossible emotional distance—just ask any woman who has placed a parent in a nursing home if it was an easy move. In the often more difficult situation where our parent remains at home, we're required to keep our feelings in check even though we're now involved in the intimacies of physical and spiritual caretaking. And when our parent dies, we're neither enabled nor encouraged, and sometimes not even expected, to mourn. Fifty-three-year-old Julia tells of a coworker asking her, "How're you doing?" two weeks after her mother's death. When she answered, "Not so well; it's really very hard," the coworker responded with a surprised expression and said, "But Julia, it's been over two weeks!" We may be well into later life before we realize we've never grieved such a passing.

Robbins made a second discovery. Most of the women she interviewed experienced more grief over the *lives* of their mothers than their actual deaths. They lamented unfulfilled dreams, unused gifts, and undereducation, and realized that as daughters they needed to mourn these.

Reflecting on a writer's block she's met while working on a script, Rita Greer Allen recognizes this is happening within herself. "I think [the block] has something to do with Mother. What?" She pursues the question in her journal, letting her thoughts and feelings about her mother surface.

"Mother has now been dead for nine years. . . . I could not ignore her, ever. I could not ignore her social standards, nor her religious beliefs. I cannot ignore her now." Still, she admits to herself, she tried. "I did evade her. That is true. I didn't, for instance, ever go to the north of England to actually see where she grew up, a hundred years ago, to experience that precarious social milieu, poor, surrounded by slum streets, where the drunken fights on Saturday nights brought on the screams for '*Pollis! The Pollis! Pollis!*' "

Now, however, during Rita's Jubilee Time, she makes the daughter's journey. She writes the story of her mother's life and recounts the choices her mother made. She recognizes how she differs from her mother, especially spiritually, but finally understands those differences. She sees that her mother, "young, passionate, her sexuality barely repressed, full of longings of all kinds," made choices that "culminated in her decision to take Jesus as her personal Savior. I believe there came a flood of ecstasy into her that could only be called holy." And though that could not and cannot be the spiritual path for her, Rita rediscovers her mother by recording these journal entries.

"Yes!" she concludes. "I can finally see how right she is. For her. So right."

THE MOTHER'S GRIEF

Daughters like us, "of a certain age," share a common tendency to relive at least some aspects of our mothers' lives. Often, it is their unfinished grieving. Sometimes our mothers were unwittingly responsible for passing their sorrow down to us; at other times, identifying with them as the same-gender parent, we took it on unbidden. Although for both mothers and daughters this may have happened at a nonconscious level, the journey of Jubilee Time is an occasion to give it back.

I remember the moment in my own life when I recognized I was carrying such a weight. Because my mother was widowed when I was 8, I grew into adolescence and early adulthood profoundly aware of her grief over my father's death. Unconsciously, I felt responsible for her sorrow; I am sure she was similarly unconscious of its effect on me. Although I was free to marry, I remained single. Then one day when I was well into my forties, a wise and compassionate therapist asked me, "Are you repeating your mother's life?" Her question hit home with such force and released so many tears that I realized I was. If she was unmarried, I would be too.

The recognition healed me; internally, I let go of a thirty-five-year-old grief that was hers, not mine. And the marriage I treasure today could not be happier.

Since that incident, I've become aware of how many other Jubilee women either relive their mothers' lives or internalize their mothers' grief. Joanne, 57, told me her experience of repeating her mother's life was almost identical to mine. And Gail, 53, told Martha Robbins:

> My mother's next-youngest sister, whom I was named after, died when she was 13 of diabetes. And I think that really put something on my mother's life. Mother talked about that all the time. You know, it's like Abigail's death was a real important something that just kept on coming down to me. And I discovered much later on that my brothers didn't know about Abigail. I was the only one who heard about her.

Fifty-two-year-old Sarah had a similar story. As a child, perceiving that her father had deprived her mother both financially and emotionally, Sarah took upon herself the role of filling the gaps in her mother's life. When she spoke of it during her Jubilee years, she said,

> It was a unique position, but ah, it was burdensome, it was very burdensome. There were times when I just wanted to be free. To have my own life, to *not* be encumbered. The guilt, of course, comes back with the understanding that can't be until that person dies. . . . That's a terrible feeling. I often felt that I was trapped and the only way out was my mother's death.

The inherited tendency for daughters to relive parts of our mothers' lives may lead us, in turn, to burden our daughters. At 50, Jane, an officer in a northeastern financial institution, reported that she discovered herself doing this when her

---

EXERCISE 4

Pause here to return to exercise 1. Reread your journal notes on your mother's life story. At this point in the ritual, add any further recollections that may have surfaced. Then add your interpretation of your mother's life, as some of the women I've quoted have done.

---

daughter returned home for the summer after her first year away at college.

"At the beginning of her vacation, I was after her every night to tell me where she was going and when she was coming in," Jane reported. "But I began to hear myself and to realize she was now a young adult. I wasn't responsible for her any longer. And I was placing on her shoulders my own worries as a mother. Because I love her dearly and treasure the special person she is, I realized I had to stop laying my fears on her, stop asking her to carry a worry that was really mine, not hers." (See Exercise 4.)

PROCESSES *IN VIA*

When we are ready to heal the brokenness in our relationships with our mothers, we find many available processes: study and conversation with other women; recording our dreams; keeping a journal; traveling home; talking with our mothers across the boundary of death. These processes "along the way" can be of special value to women orphaned early or to adopted women who want to grieve the loss of their birth mothers. The same processes can heal the sorrow that may exist in our relationships with our fathers.

Recently, I spoke with a woman whose father had died a month earlier. She said it was particularly wrenching because his death was sudden and she lived halfway across the country. The loss was deepened even more, she told me, because communication between them had always been difficult. It had taken her a year to tell him she was ending her twenty-seven-year marriage.

Now, at his death, everything she wished to say flooded her consciousness. Flying home for his funeral, she began to write him a letter—"pages and pages," she revealed. Eventually she completed the letter, and just before his funeral she slipped it into his coffin, to be buried alongside him.

Often, a central process in the daughter's journey is forgiveness, a recurring Jubilee theme. Primarily, we need to forgive our parents for being as they were and are: fallible, striving, vulnerable human beings just like us. Happily, forgiveness becomes easier as we age and find ourselves identifying with our parents. We look in a mirror and see our mother's face, or put an arm through a sweater and find her hand coming out. We treat our car exactly as our father did his and backseat-drive our children with "look-out-fors" and criticisms identical to the ones he once gave us. Having sworn we'd never treat our children as our parents treated us in adulthood, we hear ourselves calling a 40-year-old attorney to ask, "Are you wearing your boots to the office today? They're forecasting snow."

On these homely occasions, our parents' simple humanity resonates with ours. And we realize that, like ourselves, they were young once and then aged and then began to be frail. Many of them have died or will die soon. They were people, not giants. Our forgiveness can be complete.

On other occasions it's not so easy; often it may seem impossible. Some of us were abandoned, beaten, or abused by one or both of our parents. Our forgiveness in these cases includes releasing the childhood hope our parents will be other than they were. Doing this demands we be women of power, not weakness, for genuine forgiveness is difficult work, demanding courage.

But it also demands we make use of the kinds of processes and exercises central to this book: prayerful reflection, intensive breathing, thick listening, telling a life. Forgiveness counselors and therapists offer assurance that forgiveness is possible by citing women who've walked its path, sometimes by doing the interior work of journeying not *to* but *away from* abuse. When they do, they realize that the Jubilee command to "return" to our families may also take the form of returning the childhood guilt that arose from the false perception that we caused our own suffering, and releasing the childhood dream that our parents might be magically transformed. Exercise 5 provides an opportunity for such healing.

The Mythical Journey

The Jubilee command "Make the journey, every one of you, back to your place and to your people" includes at least one more pilgrimage—to women of myth who are our ancestors

Forgiveness and Healing through Imagination and Memory

If a family member, especially one of your parents, has been responsible for abusing you and causing you pain, choose that person as the focus of this exercise and prepare to engage in this practice of forgiveness and healing. Begin by sitting quietly and comfortably. Then close your eyes and attend to your breath, using a word such as *healing* or a prayer such as "Be with me now, O healing God." Repeat this word or phrase until you feel calm and ready. When you do, move through the following steps at your own pace.

Step 1: Use your imagination to take you to a place that is both safe and comfortable. Imagine this place in detail, taking time not only to see it, but to hear its sounds, touch its surfaces, and feel its surrounding comfort. Feel your own safety, calm, and readiness to forgive and to be healed. Imagine yourself accompanied by healing forces or graces, and touch these forces and graces within you.

Step 2: Now imagine the person you have come to meet as he or she approaches you. Imagine yourself as unafraid, relaxed, strong. Invite this person into your safe place, feeling your strength and wholeness as you do. Look directly at this person, noticing everything about them.

Step 3: When you are ready, begin your conversation with them, telling them the thoughts and feelings about your relationship that up to now you have left unsaid.

As you speak, refuse to deny or water down your experience, and be reverent toward the truth of it.

Step 4: When you have spoken, allow yourself to be still, and listen carefully so that you can hear what the person says back to you. Listen not only to their words, but to the truth behind their words, as you let go of blame, judgment, and resentment. Continue to breathe calmly and gently. Try to see this person in their totality, not only in the pain they have caused you.

Step 5: Be quiet for a time in each other's presence.

Step 6: After this time of quiet, if there is anything further you wish to say, take a few moments to share it.

Step 7: Now, slowly and carefully, let go of the past and again, see the person in all their wholeness, even as you feel yourself seen in all of your wholeness and maturity. In freedom, extend healing and forgiveness from within your own center toward yourself and toward this person. Call on the Healing in the universe or the God of Healing to be with you and to surround you with both healing and forgiveness.

Step 8: Say good-bye and, remaining in your safe place, watch as the person you have come to meet leaves you.

Step 9: When they have gone, return to yourself and feel the healing and forgiveness you have practiced as a mantle of goodness that covers you. Return to your breathing and get ready to open your eyes. When you are ready, open them, and continue on with your day.

Return to this exercise whenever you need to, as an opportunity to become reengaged in the process of healing.

and foremothers in a sense other than family. On this pilgrimage, we seek out archetypal figures, such as the Goddess, Medusa, the Hag (she who is holy, from the word *hagia*), and the Witch (she who brings magic to the universe), who can reveal us to ourselves.

The mythical journey is an opportunity to face and claim our entire lives: the future yet to be revealed, our present ways of being in the world, and our past memories, some brilliantly clear, others hidden and dark. The journey brings us face-to-face with our strong, benevolent self, but it also enables us to confront the monster within. When we do, we find she is a friend, not an enemy, a shadow side of us who up to now has remained under guard because her power is so great.

Medusa is a mythical figure whose story has special resonance in the lives of Jubilee women. Originally gorgeous, possessing lovely hair as the crown of her beauty, Medusa was raped by Poseidon, the Lord of the Sea. She was the one punished, however. The feature for which she's universally remembered, her hair, was turned into revolting serpents. Like so many women before and since, the victim was blamed and those near her averted their faces, unable to gaze at the serpents. As with too many older women, a society she did not create decreed she was no longer beautiful and punished her for losing her younger self. Even Medusa herself turned away from her own image.

The work of the mythical journey back to place and people is the opposite of Medusa's tale: we must gaze at what may terrify us, especially if that is the fact of growing old, and turn it into a symbol of new life. After gazing at serpents, for example, we eventually see they are the intertwined symbols in the caduceus, the medical image of healing and hope.

Inanna and Erishkegal are two mythical figures who also reveal us to ourselves. Their story, dating from early in the second millennium B.C.E., is one of the oldest surviving women's tales we have, appropriate for this ritual because it recounts a mature woman's journey. The story tells of the pilgrimage of Queen Inanna to the underworld ruled by her sister, Erishkegal. Found in Sumerian legend, the story is a first rendering of the descent of the Goddess, a forerunner to the Babylonian myth of Ishtar several centuries later and the Greek myth of Demeter and Persephone that appears in the next millennium. Unlike the young maiden Persephone, however, tricked by Pluto and carried off to the underworld, Inanna initiates the journey herself, and makes it for her own reasons. In complete control of her actions, she even leaves behind identical messages for three of her gods telling how she expects them to rescue her if she fails to return. An ancient Sumerian chant extols her:

> The Goddess from the "great above," she set her mind
>   toward the "great below,"
> Inanna, from the "great above," she set her mind
>   toward the "great below."
> My lady abandoned heaven, abandoned earth, to the
>   nether world she descended,
> Abandoned lordship, abandoned ladyship, to the
>   nether world she descended.

Inanna is in search of Erishkegal, her "sister," the monstrous Queen of the Underworld. The journey takes her not only back to her origins but down, into the deep places of earth and self.

While Inanna is gone, the part of the earth that is her domain in the "great above" becomes barren. As she journeys she passes through a series of gates, and at each is stripped of a divine power or royal prerogative until finally she is brought in "naked and bowed low" before the throne of Erishkegal. There she is killed by the "eyes of death" and "the word which tortures the spirit." Her corpse is tied to a large stake and left to decompose, but during this time, Er-

---

EXERCISE 6

Meeting Inanna and Erishkegal

In the mythical journey of Jubilee women, Inanna and Erishkegal represent the encounter between pairs of sisters within us, such as youth and age, heaven and earth, life and death. Begin this exercise by using both their names as a mantra: breathe in on *Inanna,* breathe out on *Erishkegal.* In, out, in, out, "Inanna, Erishkegal, Inanna, Erishkegal," for at least ten breaths, or until you have become still enough to listen to their counterparts within you. Then take time to meditate on the following:

1. At each threshold Inanna passes over, she is stripped of one of her attributes. Pause to list or draw three to five attributes, especially youthful qualities, no longer yours.

ishkegal also is suffering, and is described as lying ill. After three days, rescuers finally arrive in the underworld, save Inanna, and return her to the land of the living, where her lost attributes are restored.

Each woman accompanying the Inanna within herself as she travels to Erishkegal's realm will interpret different aspects of the journey in ways unique to her; Exercise 6 presents this opportunity.

2. After three days, Inanna's attributes are restored to her. Take the same three to five attributes you've just noted and list or draw what they've changed into now that you live in Jubilee Time.

3. What is a "great above" in your life? What is a "great below"?

4. What does the three-day period represent for you? What does the stake represent for you?

5. What is a now barren or unfruitful part of your life, something to which you must bid farewell?

6. What is a powerful, passionate, unique part of your present life to which you must now bid welcome?

7. What "underworlds," represented by Erishkegal, are places in your life to which you must journey as you move through your Jubilee years?

8. Now imagine a conversation between the Inanna and Erishkegal within you. Where and how do they call you to die? Where and how do they call you to live?

At the same time that we interpret the Inanna story personally, we are wise to be aware that certain parts of this story have meaning for all Jubilee women, creating bonds between us, even as they did between the two mythical sisters. Our Jubilee journey begins, for example, with the passage across the threshold of age. It continues as we accept this new era in our lives. With menopause over, or about to end, we are apparently facing barrenness too—at least in a physical sense—although that can be the prelude to another kind of fruitfulness. We may feel stripped of earlier powers, especially the powers of youth, and when brought into the presence of Erishkegal—who represents our hidden selves—may feel naked and bowed low, particularly if osteoporosis is curving our spine.

But barrenness, the end of youthful power, nakedness, and being bowed low have other meanings. Barrenness can be the opportunity to let the land lie fallow and to deepen our hallowing. It can provide occasions for cultivating spiritual simplicity, letting go of possessions and prerogatives that no longer have meaning in our lives. The loss of the regal powers of youth can attune us to the power of the inner elder who brings to spirituality what often is lacking in the image of God: the female, the shadow, the wanderer, the crone.

In addition, although nakedness is often associated with dying, it also symbolizes birth and brand-new life. For Jubilee women, such life burgeons today, as we leave constricting roles and outdated notions of female elderhood in order to be free. And bowing low is the posture of reverence, the posture of prayer, the attitude of waiting upon the moment in order to savor the next miracle time will bring.

Most of all, however, this mythical journey provides insight into the underworld and the chance to confront the dying, darkness, and mystery within it as familiar and necessary companions, not monsters. Women past 50 and 60 and 70 and 80, we know our lives are places of intersection between seen and unseen, pain and joy, life and death, and we take this knowledge wherever we go, enabling us to caress every new day with what Sylvia Ashton-Warner once called "a light enough touch."

The journeys we take now, into our later years, are meetings with our mythical ancestors. But they are also a chance to encounter unknown parts of ourselves associated with age: ourselves as hag and crone, the woman of "wise blood"; ourselves as Medusa, from whom others turn away; ourselves as Sancta Sophia, figure of holy but hard-earned wisdom. If we submit to the chaos and pain the stake of death represents, we can become whole. And out of our wholeness, we can create new pathways into the land of aging that bear our footprints. In our continuing travels along those pathways, we can discover personal attributes unused until now or dormant since our girlhood. We can offer the world new visions of what it means to grow old. And we can model and demonstrate those visions everywhere, even as they guide us into becoming true Jubilarians, transformed by encounters with the underworld, with dying, and with the coming of age.

Five

*T*AKING *I*NVENTORY

You shall count off seven weeks of years, seven times seven years, so that the period of seven weeks of years gives forty-nine years.

Lev. 25:8

One morning as we ended an academic advisory session in my office, Donna, my 33-year-old advisee, stood up, thanked me, and started to leave. Then she turned and said, "By the way, Maria, there's something I've been meaning to ask you." She hesitated, giving me a semi-embarrassed grin. But the grin faded and her face became serious as she asked, "How did you get to be the way you are?"

Several times since, a young woman—usually a student or an instructor at the start of her teaching career—has asked me the same question, using the same words. That first time, a neophyte at responding, I was at the beginning of my Jubilee years. So I went into considerable detail describing my life to poor Donna. But when it happened again, I said to myself, "Dummy! The question isn't about *you.*" When one woman asks another how she got to be as she is, the younger one is interested in learning about *herself.* She's been watching and observing—as we all do—and found something in the way one of us older women acts that she wants to imitate. Even if she's in her thirties or forties, she's saying, "I'd like to be like *you* when I grow up."

As we begin this ritual we turn the question on ourselves. It's now time to figure out exactly how we did get to be the way we are. The Jubilee command to "count off" a period of fifty years slows us down so we might take inventory. Beginning in our fifties, but with even more intensity as the decades follow, we mull over the questions: Where have I been? Where am I now? Where am I going? We examine not only those things that have meaning *in* our lives but also the meaning *of* our lives.

The focus of Jubilee's command to "count off" at the fiftieth year is not so much the fiftieth year as it is the counting. This counting is mirrored in several related counsels in Leviticus that tell the Jubilarian to examine possessions—If you buy property, keep it till the year of Jubilee; then release and return it; to exercise power with care—You have authority, but never use it harshly; and to explore human relationships—Be sure to care for your kin; help them if they're needy; take them in. It becomes clear early on that the counting and assessing in this ritual are tasks of the soul and spirit, not arithmetical ones.

Taking Inventory, the fifth Jubilee ritual, provides an opportunity to do this spiritual work. The things we cherish, the ways we characteristically use power, and the persons we've loved are what shape our identity and make us who we are. It's time to examine them in detail.

A Natural Jubilee Moment

Reflection and accounting are a natural part of Jubilee Time. At the simplest level, many of us make a will at this stage of life, with the footdraggers admitting they're thinking about it or feeling guilty because they haven't. We sign medical directives authorizing or refusing certain medical procedures in case of illness. Recognizing that the sunset of life is approaching, we give away cherished possessions and property to our children, relatives, and friends, whether that's a lakeside cabin, furniture, silverware, jewelry, or treasured mementos. Or we say to someone special, "When I'm gone, I'd like you to have this."

Exercise 1

Blessing Our Things

In the third Jubilee ritual, we reflected on our role as priests. One of the things priests do is lay hands on someone or something, to bless them and honor their sacred character.

This exercise is directed toward doing this with the things that are sacred to us, admitting our genuine relation with them and affirming their sacredness in our lives. It is an exercise of particular importance before a move or before a garage or tag sale, giving us a chance to say good-bye. Read the exercise through first, then follow the directions.

Moving from a large house to a small apartment, or moving nearer other family members after widowhood or divorce, we pare down. Having sold her house, 66-year-old Cora is holding a bittersweet garage sale, painfully letting go of what seems too much like the detritus of her life. Seventy-year-old Marguerite, her neighbor, has decided to give the two cappuccino machines she's stashed in her basement to her daughters. When my 83-year-old mother stopped living alone and moved in with my brother's family, she gave me her antique desk, her Czechoslovakian china, and her Waterford cocktail shaker; she gave Tom our father's World War I medals and the Bavarian figurines and the vases-become-lampstands from our childhood home.

1. Move through your house at a reduced pace, very, very slowly.
2. Be prepared to stop before at least ten objects from your everyday life that you want to acknowledge and bless. These might include piano, bed, television, dog dish, lamps, candle holders, earrings—anything at all.
3. Pause before the particular object you've chosen.
4. Extend your hands toward the object and then rest them on it for several seconds.
5. As you do, say, "I bless you and I thank you for all you've meant to me."
6. Move on and repeat this with each treasured object until you've completed your blessings.

Such paring down is a ritual that symbolizes other, more personal parings such as loss and death, and nudges Jubilee women into the distillation process that characterizes aging. But the paring also spurs us to summarize and account for our lives in a way that helps us grasp their meaning. Inventory illuminates identity. (See Exercise 1.)

A TRIAD AT THE CENTER

This ritual centers on a trinity of concerns: *possessions, power,* and *human relationships.* These are basic to any spiritual inventory, but I have selected them here because they stem from roots found in both religious life and feminist writing.

The religious roots lie in criteria and practices common to religious orders of women, whether these orders are made up of Buddhist sisters or Catholic nuns. For centuries, women in such orders have taken vows, or dedicated themselves to lives of poverty, obedience, and chastity. And in *Three Guineas,* Virginia Woolf's feminist classic written when she was 56, we find almost identical criteria: women's lives must include, says Woolf, the refusal to be separated from poverty, derision, and chastity.

Spiritual traditions of poverty lead us to examine our relation to possessions. Woolf defined poverty as having enough money to live on, enough to be independent or interdependent, and nothing more. In another classic work, she put this at "a room of one's own and five hundred pounds a year." As a facet of life in women's orders, poverty as an ideal reminds women to question whether we pursue having and owning so avidly that we forget being and sitting still, forget hallowing, forget Jubilee's command to let the land lie fallow.

I have quite a bit of experience here. For twenty years, as a Sister of St. Joseph in the 1950s and 1960s, I was under a vow of poverty. Today many sisters in religious orders use the term *simplicity* instead of *poverty,* aware through their own advocacy for the poor that theirs isn't genuine poverty, which is actually an evil, not a blessing.

In those days of being under the vow, we took only personal clothing and two books—the New Testament and *The Imitation of Christ*—when we moved from one convent to another. We held everything else in common. We had no money in our purses because we didn't have purses. Our strict external poverty made for rich interior freedom. Today, when I visit my Buddhist friend Chung-ok Lee at her temple in Manhattan, I'm brought back to those years. Although Chung's is an Asian tradition, and she was born on the other side of the world, she lives in a community of women with ideals that are identical to the ones I knew.

Obedience, the second criterion, refers to power and acknowledges our capacity to act for both good and evil. Ideally, adult obedience, even for nuns, isn't to other people (let alone the Pope). It is to the laws of our own being and the inner commands of the Spirit to use our power justly and humanely. Someone once told me that the word *obedience* stems from the Latin *ab audire*—to hold one's ear against the earth in order to hear its instructions. I discovered later that was inaccurate etymologically, but I don't think it was wrong. My friend Chung refers to this obedient listening as responding to the Buddha nature within her, holding her own ear against the promptings coming from within her essential self.

Virginia Woolf's derision is about power too. She explains how derision alerts women to the seductions and pomposity of power, and counsels laughter—even laughter at ourselves— as far more important than placement on a pedestal. When we imagine ourselves higher than we are, "above" some things or even above some people, it's time to laugh at ourselves and be gently derisive. Laughter reminds us to take our power seriously but not solemnly.

Chastity leads us to examine our relationships. It calls us to reverence our bodies, especially as they grow soft, sere, and slow, and to acknowledge the goodness of our sexuality. Rather than deny sexuality, an ideal of chastity affirms our capacities for love and intimacy and refuses to separate sex from that love or to reduce sex to "use" alone. As an ideal, chastity reminds us to extend the same respect to others that we want for ourselves.

Putting a spin on the word, Virginia Woolf says the practice of chastity means we refuse to prostitute our *minds*. When you have enough to live on, she counsels, don't sell (today we'd say "sell out") your thoughts, your convictions, your attitudes. Keep your mind as well as your body chaste—free from anyone else's ownership.

Finally, Woolf used a fourth criterion to hone our relations to possessions, power, and people: *freedom from unreal loyalties*. She counseled ridding ourselves of national pride, religious pride, family pride, and those innumerable false loyalties—including racial pride and class pride—that spring from them and keep women separated from ourselves, one another, and the universe.

POSSESSIONS

Examining our relations to possessions helps us ground this ritual in physical reality. "Is it easier," asks one woman, "to find the perfect man or the perfect handbag?" Counting the number of shoes or purses in our closets, we realize we can become addicted—not to the objects themselves, but to the process of accumulating them. So this ritual, where we inventory our things, can attune us to personal addictions. Conversely, and as a part of our spirituality, it can also alert us to the lack of possessions—in the form of economic insecurity—that frightens too many older women in our society.

Virginia Woolf's question is the key to this first level of taking inventory: "Do I have enough to live on?" Facing her later years, 58-year-old Irene tells me she loses many hours of sleep these days attempting—with her pocket calculator in the small morning hours—to answer this question. Being widowed and left without a job or savings underlies her fear and her insomnia. For other women, the scary circumstances may be divorce or an unjust divorce settlement, physical or mental disability, or forced retirement. Still others are frightened by the following data about older women in the United States:

- Over seventy percent of the nearly four million persons over 65 living in poverty are women
- Fewer than one older woman in five currently receives any pension income outside of Social Security
- Millions of midlife and older women have no health insurance or, like me, not yet 65, are dependent on their husbands'

Before she retired, one of my correspondents' professional work centered on such issues, and involvement in them had eventually paid off for her. "As a single woman of 75," she wrote, "life—and being one of the earliest employed in the field—has taught me the importance of financial planning." Although a "Preparing for Retirement" seminar may not appeal to us in our late forties or early fifties, it may be a good way to lay the groundwork for future Jubilee accounting. A clear view of our financial situation might not seem to be a topic of spirituality, but it couldn't be more central. Crucial to

EXERCISE 2

For Ready Reference

At your convenience, but no later than the end of the month, write to the following for information and/or membership details. AARP accepts people at 50; there are no member age limits for OWL or the Gray Panthers.

American Association of Retired Persons
1909 K Street, NW
Washington, DC 20049

Ask also for their publications *Mastering Your Money* and *A Guide to Understanding Your Pension Plan.*

Gray Panthers. Membership Department
2025 Pennsylvania Avenue, NW, Suite 821
Washington, DC 20077-2668

feeding the spirit is feeding, clothing, and housing the body over the long haul.

In the same vein, although we might not consider ourselves joiners, memberships in AARP, the Gray Panthers, and particularly the Older Women's League (OWL is the only organization specifically concerned with aging *women,* especially our finances) are marvelous 50-and-over birthday gifts to ourselves

Older Women's League
666 Eleventh Street NW, #700
Washington, DC 20001-4512

"The Medical Directive," published by the American Medical Association in 1990 as a supplement to the *Harvard Medical School Health Letter,* June 1990. Available for $1 and a stamped, self-addressed envelope from:

Harvard Medical School Health Letter
164 Longwood Avenue, fourth floor
Boston, MA 02115

National Pension Assistance Project
918 Sixteenth Street NW, Suite 704
Washington, DC 20006

and others. They provide resources that teach us how to handle our finances and become vocal advocates for all older women. (See Exercise 2.)

Another way to examine possessions is to identify those treasures whose loss would devastate you. I'm still lamenting a medallion stolen when my car was broken into one Thanksgiving. Gabriel had brought it back to me from Rome long before we were married and it was as powerful a symbol of our love as my wedding ring. Fran, an Australian friend, told me that the first things she grabbed when she became aware of flames in her flat were her photograph albums. And one night on the old Johnny Carson show, singer Tony Martin talked about a robbery in the home he shared with his wife, dancer Cyd Charisse. Although they'd lost many possessions, none had hurt more than the loss of one pair of worn ballet shoes, the first Cyd had used dancing as a professional.

In exercises such as Exercise 3, many of us find that with few exceptions, those things we cherish most are not the ones that cost most. We're rarely in Queen Elizabeth's boots, having to save the paintings in Windsor Castle. Instead, our most treasured possessions have symbolic value: if I show you my treasure, you'll understand my heart. As the poet Virgil wrote centuries ago, there are "tears to things," *lacrimae rerum*. The tears arise from the poignancy attached to things that remind us of those who've given us those things, even as they interpret for us who we are now. We must honor the objects as well as the memories.

As we age, most of us grant increasing pride of place to health and the life of our body, mind, and senses. We acknowledge their fragility. "Since I live at a retirement home," says Kitty, 75, "I have near me examples of what old age potentially can bring in physical and mental powers' deterioration." Those

EXERCISE 3

Where Your Treasure Is

Begin by sitting quietly, lighting a candle, and concentrating on your breath. Inhale and exhale ten or twelve times, using the mantra "my treasure, my heart." When you feel yourself centered, reflect on the following:

1. If you've ever been evacuated, or in a fire, what was the first thing you grabbed?
2. If you haven't, what do you think you'd grab? Why?
3. How many treasures do you actually have? One? Two? Several? Which hold the most meaning for you?
4. As you've grown older, how have your attitudes toward your possessions changed?

Conclude the exercise by giving thanks for all the possessions of your life.

of us who were ill as children or young women—Evelyn, now 61, with rheumatic fever; Sandy, now 60, with nephritis; Kathy, now 58, with asthma—don't need to be told good health is a treasure. The rest of us learn to reverence it as we age, pausing regularly in rituals such as this to inventory it, and hoping to hold on to it into our final years.

One pair of treasures not to be overlooked or underestimated are our fellow creatures on planet Earth and planet Earth itself. Sixty-four-year-old Emily captures delight in the first in a recent note to me. About to take off on an Elderhostel trip to the Galapagos Islands ("It's the cheapest way to go"), she writes from Florida:

> It is early morning. I am sitting in a bay window where I have my desk. I look out on a pond—golf

---

EXERCISE 4

An Environmental Legacy

The following is most appropriately done in a group or a circle meeting regularly. It concerns one of the most cherished "possessions" of all human beings—planet Earth with all its facets.

Choose at least five of the earth's gifts that have special meaning for you. These might include a constellation, summer rain, a moon phase, the Pacific Ocean, a nearby mountain, a dirt path, a chrysanthemum, a favorite tree.

1. Draw, paint, photograph, or find a picture—perhaps in a magazine—of the first of the earth's gifts you've se-

course—sky—where *eagles* fly!! Snowy egrets do mating prances under my window, and huge turtles bask in the sun on the bank of the pond. And last week, an alligator swam by when my children were here.

The second treasure is the earth itself with its stars, rain, ever-changing seasons. Few older women are more eloquent in their appreciation of these than May Sarton, a leading candidate for poet laureate of Jubilee women and a maker of gardens, tiller of soil, singer of the earth's glories. In *At Seventy*, she recognizes these most cherished possessions and the many

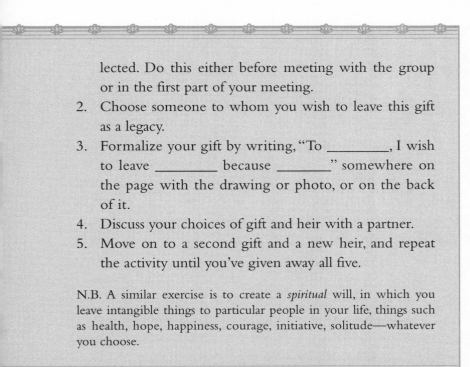

lected. Do this either before meeting with the group or in the first part of your meeting.

2. Choose someone to whom you wish to leave this gift as a legacy.

3. Formalize your gift by writing, "To _____, I wish to leave _____ because _____" somewhere on the page with the drawing or photo, or on the back of it.

4. Discuss your choices of gift and heir with a partner.

5. Move on to a second gift and a new heir, and repeat the activity until you've given away all five.

N.B. A similar exercise is to create a *spiritual* will, in which you leave intangible things to particular people in your life, things such as health, hope, happiness, courage, initiative, solitude—whatever you choose.

forms they take. "Yesterday was a great wallow of weather," she writes, "a wonderful mass of dark clouds over a tumbled, rough ocean, with towers of spray flashing up at the end of the field, high wind, an exhilarating sense of autumn. And suddenly the leaves are at their peak here, and at every turn scarlet and orange and saffron light up the road."

Most of us aren't gifted with her eloquence or with Emily's, but all of us can share their passion. Perhaps a resolution arising from this ritual might be to allow no day to go by without counting up, acknowledging, and giving thanks for the earth, water, wind, and sky continually blessing our lives. (See Exercise 4.)

POWER

In this ritual, power is the second subject of inventory. As we count off the past fifty, sixty, or seventy years, here is a time to pause and give thanks for contemporary movements for human liberation, including the worldwide women's movement. Largely as a result of them, *power* in our time has ceased being a dirty word. Taught for centuries that there's virtue in giving up power, even in powerlessness—especially in so-called spiritual instructions—Jubilee women are now resisting such dicta on a global scale.

Tutored by wise old women such as Elizabeth Janeway, we're learning to draw on what she calls "powers of the weak," capacities usually associated with poor or "insignificant" people, including children, the old, women, and, in societies where being white automatically confers privilege, persons of color. These are powers such as *disbelief,* the refusal to accept "truths" about your unimportance or second-class status, and *bonding,* coming together in the belief that although one or two may not be able to achieve much, the old marching song is right: "two and two and fifty" can "make a million" who'll tear down ageist, sexist, classist, and racist systems by exercising a third power, *joint action.*

Today's Jubilarians assess power in a changed social context because during our lives, the meaning of power has shifted. I remember the day in the mid-1970s when this knowledge first struck me. I'd been asked to lead a seminar on the power of teaching in Chicopee, Massachusetts, and decided to begin with a go-around. I asked each person present—we were all women—to fill in the blanks by saying, "My name is _____ and for me, power is _____." We came to a white-haired woman who was obviously the oldest in our group. She told us her name, Frances, and then she said: "I don't know what power is. All my life, men have defined it. It's only now, at 78, that I'm part of the work of giving it meaning."

I think she was right. Historically, men who held power defined it; now that we women have been empowered to create our own meanings for it, we've come at power differently. Consider two of the world's foremost thinkers. Max Weber says power is the probability that people acting in a social relation can carry out their will despite resistance. In contrast, Hannah Arendt says power is the capacity to agree on a particular action in uncoerced communication. Arendt's stress on the consensual, cooperative, nonconfrontational nature of power reminds us it doesn't have to be synonymous with force or violence.

Religious traditions have compounded the ambiguity and complexity of our relationship to power. Like other patriarchal institutions, religions have shown a chilling capacity for exercising the power of destruction: the witch hunts of the Christian Inquisition and the suttee of Hinduism—where a widow is burned on her husband's pyre when he dies—come to my mind. At the same time, religions have preached the renunciation of power as another kind of power: St. Paul's kenosis ("emptying") to describe Jesus's sacrifice; Reverend Martin Luther King, Jr.'s nonviolence; Gandhi's satyagraha or "truth force." Women are understandably skeptical of religious talk about power; we've suffered too much from action that diametrically opposed the talk.

For me, that means that when I poll women on power now, I don't expect the definitive word on it. No single one of us knows everything about power—we're feeling our way, refashioning its meaning together. The etymology of the word suggests a starting point: power is *capacity* and *ability*. More specific to our Jubilee mandate, power is our capacity to act, both receptively and proactively. As receivers, we are contemplatives—listening thickly to the world, one another, ourselves, and to the Holiness dwelling in all of these. We exercise this receptive power as we approach new thresholds or take time for hallowing.

As doers, we exercise power actively, especially in proclaiming liberty and making necessary journeys. Although we may find using power difficult, even an "unlearning to not speak," in Marge Piercy's phrase, such unlearning releases us from the fear of using power, particularly as we age and realize we have nothing to lose when we do.

Although we're still working on its precise meaning, women are exercising power today in wonderful ways. I once heard a woman who'd gone to Peru with a women's rights group talk about their work there. The group was particularly concerned with the extent of wife battering and abuse in one area, and with teaching women how to use their power in response. Weekends were especially violent times for many of the women; their husbands would receive their paychecks and spend much of it on liquor before going home and beating the women. The rights group taught the women the power residing in bonding and joint action, and enlisted their children in the effort too. If a man arrived home and began beating his wife, one or several of the children would blow a whistle and then grab a metal pot and a piece of pipe, rush outside the house, and begin banging the pot for all in the village to hear. At the sound, the women of the village dropped whatever they were doing and joined the din, descending on the offending husband and pulling him off his wife with strength and ferocity. That ended the practice of wife beating in the area and heightened the women's awareness of their power.

I've found the circle go-around is still one of the richest ways to explore power's meaning for women. But now, when we come together, I ask women to say their entire names (childhood nicknames, several marriage names, whatever)—a power in itself, that naming—and then tell the rest of us one of their powers.

The first response is often hesitant. At a recent workshop I led, it began with, "I can use a computer," "I can dance," "I can cook and bake and preserve," "I can drive a car," "I can write a poem." But as the environment became relaxed and we got to know one another, the next go-around went deeper. Other answers started to tumble out, as varied and sacred as the spirits of the women speaking: "Courage," "Putting up with pain," "Telling people I'm needy," "Facing death."

Eventually, we trusted one another enough to share our deepest personal stories. When I asked—or they asked one

EXERCISE 5

Taking a Power Inventory

Begin this exercise by breathing regularly, centering your-self, and using the one word *power* as a mantra. When you've become calm, take time to inventory your responses to the following questions.

1. If you were in a circle of women (or if you are) and the go-around came to you, how would you fill in the blank in "For me, power is _____"?
2. Recall an incident in the last ten years when you exer-cised the power of disbelief, saying something along the lines of "I don't believe that, not anymore."

another—for a story describing an exercise of power, the revelations began. "I was widowed at 37 and raised six daughters and a son," said 66-year-old Mary proudly. "I've survived the coal-black night of depression—so far," said 50-year-old Rosemary. "I gained my black belt in karate," said 60-year-old Leah. "I saw my son through four years of AIDS," wept 76-year-old Carrie. Such practices are ways to reveal our powers not only to others, but to ourselves—of-ten for the first time. As we speak we realize that the powers we've developed to heal ourselves are powers that also may heal the world. (See Exercise 5.)

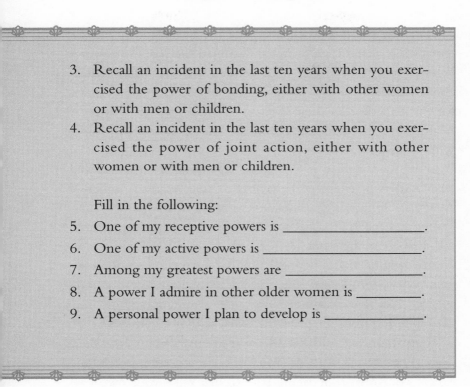

3. Recall an incident in the last ten years when you exercised the power of bonding, either with other women or with men or children.

4. Recall an incident in the last ten years when you exercised the power of joint action, either with other women or with men or children.

Fill in the following:

5. One of my receptive powers is _____.

6. One of my active powers is _____.

7. Among my greatest powers are _____.

8. A power I admire in other older women is _____.

9. A personal power I plan to develop is _____.

HUMAN RELATIONSHIPS

Gloria Steinem once commented, "We are all trained to be female impersonators." She was referring to the way we have absorbed culturally imposed definitions of womanhood: what *real* women look like (tall, thin), what they act like (servants), how they think ("I'm not really important"). Internalizing those doctrines alienated us from who we actually were. Inundated by instruction on how to be not just female but "feminine," we squelched many of our natural impulses and impersonated behavior we imagined to be "correct."

Happily, some of us escaped. But the power of the indoc-
trination revealed itself to me as I studied the questionnaires I
received and realized that what women celebrated most often
about Jubilee Time was the end of impersonation. Sometimes
for the first time in their lives, they could give priority to a
relationship that had often troubled them: their relationship
with *themselves.*

For Noel, Jubilee is a time of "liberation from the clean,
neat borders of expected behaviors or rules made by others."
At 50, she contrasted her earlier years with what was now happening in her life. "I'm coming to know myself, to forgive myself. I'm accepting—but not excusing—myself and my faults,
acknowledging my gifts, and learning to trust the small, inner
voice of wisdom I carry, the one I was encultured to ignore
as 'nonsensical' or 'nonprovable.' That voice comes from my
very soul, and from the place the Spirit within me resides."

Fifty-four-year-old Eileen, an elementary-school teacher
from Pennsylvania, agreed. "You can't *own* anything in this life
except your own soul. Being true to that self—your own nature—is all that's important. That's your real union with the
Divine." From Osaka, 54-year-old Michiko wrote, "There's a
gradual process in growing older that's brought me into
knowing who I am. I'm able to accept myself as I am—and
love myself. I don't have to worry how I look or what others
think of me." She admitted that living up to this "was sometimes lonely and took energy," but giving up and letting go of
the false images was the way to build "better relationships,
better bridges."

Opal, a 52-year-old Cheyenne from New Mexico, linked
this self-relatedness to relations with others: "We've got to love
ourselves before we can extend love to others." That done,

many women made essential connections between becoming one's own woman and needing companions on the journey. Mary, who at 65 named the best thing about growing old as "having a chance to use my knowledge to finish life with a bang, not a whimper," added, "But I need more community— I'll have to search this out." And 78-year-old Catherine praised such community, writing, "As I age, relationships take on added importance, particularly with the people I see on a regular basis."

Among these relationships are those with our children. Older adulthood is a period when many of us who are parents have to adjust to a more grown-up relation with our daughters and sons. This can be a difficult transition, but it can also be a chance to repair old wounds and resentments. Better than that, Jubilee Time can be the period when we and our adult children eventually become strong, faithful friends.

Friendship often surfaced in the inventories. Florence, on leave from her job in Zimbabwe for a visit to the States, discussed its importance, even though she noted that making friends sometimes involved risk. "Still," she wrote, "it's better to err trusting and loving others than be afraid to trust or love because I might be disappointed." That attitude had taught her to try "to make the first move in reaching out to another." At the same age—57—Joyce agreed, adding, "Friendships need to be nurtured and all friendships, even if they're few, are precious." In her sixties, Helen didn't seem to mind the risks in making friends. A retired secretary, she wrote, "Life has taught me to *be* someone's friend instead of looking for one."

It was in comments such as Kitty's that the issue of sexuality in relations surfaced. From her store of seventy-five years of wisdom, she noted:

I have come to know that, even though the fires are
banked and I am no longer at the mercy of the emotional swings of adolescence and menopause, I am still
aware of my sexuality; that it can be an important part
of my identity as a person and add vitality to my relationships with others. Intimacy based on mutuality becomes increasingly precious to me.

No longer pretending to be sexually reserved because it's not
"feminine" to show sexual desire, older women—at least the
more outspoken of us—are addressing this issue head on. Betty
Friedan describes being at a meeting where gerontologists
were affirming active sex lives for women into our seventies
and eighties, when Maggie Kuhn, the Gray Panthers' founder,
stood up and cut to the chase. Noting statistics indicating there
were as many as ten widows for every widower in the country
today, Kuhn suggested that if an older woman was going to
have sex, it would have to be with a younger man, or some-
body else's husband, or another woman, or with herself. She
ended by describing a commune she lived in, where she'd
made a nonexclusive contract for sex with a younger, married
lover, rather than give it up.

That may or may not be the route for us, but we would
be perpetuating female impersonation if we gave up our
search for human intimacy or our right to it. Sometimes the
intimacy will be physical, but it need not be. The women
who spoke to this issue for me widened the definition of intimacy beyond sex alone. Mona, a Maori woman from New
Zealand, said one of the best things about growing older was
a "different kind of love toward my partner," whereas Sarah,
56, gave more detail.

These years have offered me many opportunities to deepen my relationship with my husband, Bob. We have much more time together now that the years of active parenting are over. We're fortunate to have the financial means to enjoy vacations and weekend retreats together. I feel that there has been a blossoming of my own sexuality and a greater yearning for intimacy. My sexual life is more satisfying than at any other time in my life. I also feel a much greater sense of companionship in my marriage.

Regina, 54, described a similar set of opportunities, and took delight in describing the loveliness of "building a fire and lighting candles for my husband and me every Friday evening," and of "making love with deeper levels of passion." And at 65 Velma, affirming age as a time for "freedom to be *me,*" added, "Marriage has become richer now that the roles of mother, housekeeper, wife, and teacher no longer predominate." She was among the many women in the process of discovering that, as 57-year-old Sylvia explained, "my husband and I share *more* now than our children. We're learning how to be best friends."

Recently retired from nursing, and both amused and sobered by the milestone of her first Social Security check, 62-year-old Pat reminisced with me on all the relations of her life up to now. "From Frank [her physician husband] I've learned the meaning of persons. He's always said of patients that everyone is someone's daughter, someone's grandfather, someone's friend, each with their own story. They're never the liver, the spinal injury, the coronary." She went on, "From my mother I learned how to endure. She taught me that with humor and with laughter. From my friend Helen, I learned about another place: the spiritual life. From Kay I've learned serenity. She's a doctor's wife too, so we have much in common. Frank, of

---

Ending Female Impersonation

Female impersonators are adult women who act according to someone else's rules. In this exercise we reflect on some of these rules, and create our own similar or contrasting ones. Again, we may do this alone, but it may be more fun to do it in a group.

Step 1:

1. A female impersonator always attends to others first; a real woman _____.
2. A female impersonator never raises her voice; a real woman _____.
3. A female impersonator follows orders; a real woman _____.
4. A female impersonator gives in graciously; a real woman _____.
5. A female impersonator sends her sons and daughters to war; a real woman _____.
6. A female impersonator never shows anyone the real color of her hair; a real woman _____.

course, continues to teach me." Echoing Sylvia, she concluded, "Perhaps we are now best friends as well as lovers."

Based on Pat's simple inventory, we can make our own.

---

7. A female impersonator always covers her face and eyes with makeup; a real woman _____.

8. A female impersonator is always "fixing" her body; a real woman _____.

9. A female impersonator knows that any man can make better decisions than she can; a real woman _____
_____.

10. A female impersonator gets her power, authority, and sense of herself from "important" people; a real woman

_____.

Step 2. Using these ten starters as models, make up at least five more statements clarifying the meaning of "female impersonator" for yourself.

Step 3. Take special note of the statements that triggered strong feelings for you—of avoidance and resentment, of excitement and delight. These can be sources of self-understanding.

Step 4. Share your responses with a group of friends, including examples of when and how they've applied to your life and experience. Decide what they imply for you as a Jubilee woman.

"From _____ I learned _____" is a good formula. It's a way of summing up our own lives in terms of our relations and what they've given us up to now.

CONTINUING THE INVENTORY

A powerful truth emerges as this ritual continues to reveal new facets of our identities: those identities are works in progress that need an entire lifetime to complete. For even as we inventory our lives thus far, further challenges scratch at us from inside our souls, propelling us toward the future. Scouting the terrain of the land of aging in which we now dwell, we recognize that this land poses new questions, provoked not by the past but by the decades ahead. "What remains for me to do?" we now ask. "How shall I use the powers I've named? What is the work of the rest of my life?"

The Jubilee women I've spoken to, like all women, have a long history of work. Some held paid jobs throughout their adult lives and many have them still; others' major work was at home, doing the caretaking society continues to assign largely to us. Many have done both.

In Jubilee Time, another kind of work manifests itself, work implied by taking inventory: letting go, claiming power, creating community, loving one another unto death and beyond. Finally, we are prepared to center on the *real* work of our lives, to which we may have given only sporadic attention thus far: re-creating women's identity by moving consciously and with grace into maturity, aging, old age, and death.

Fifty-seven-year-old Anne Ness of Saratoga, California, spins a metaphor that describes this vocation.

I feel I have been given an incredible space of time, freedom, wisdom, and opportunity to live more fully in this, the final third of my life. It is my intention to use this opportunity to create a work of art, a magnum opus of my life. This is a luxury my mother's generation didn't have and something I can model for those who follow me, as I invite others to join me on this journey.

The circumstances of our individual lives will provide the medium of this work of art, conditioning whether it will be—continuing Anne's metaphor—a painting, a sculpture, a dance, a poem, a drama. The work will be shaped by where we live and with whom, as well as by our particular thresholds, hallowings, journeys, freedoms, and inventories. It will include new work that knocks at the door of our future, asking, "May I come in?" Its extent will depend on gains and losses, health and time.

This is, of course, work already begun, although we may have been too busy to notice. But in Jubilee Time, as we slow down to acknowledge and focus on it, we will realize its fundamentally spiritual character. Working in concert with women across the country and across the planet, we will know that we have been called to fashion a woman's whole life by the Creative One who made us "in the beginning." Continuing this ritual to the end of our lives through our artistry and our power, we shall come closer and closer to discovering how we got to be as we are.

Six

*T*ELLING *O*UR *S*TORY

I, your God, brought you out of the land of Egypt, to give you the land of Canaan.

Lev. 25:38

As I completed the first half of my life and prepared to enter my Jubilee years, I discovered Lilith, Eve's predecessor in the Garden of Eden. It seems God created Adam and Lilith in the beginning, but Lilith was too uppity for Adam. When he said, "I'll have my figs now, Lilith," she tended to say, "You can get them yourself." When he asked, "Are you going to clean up the garden?" she answered, "No, it's your turn." Annoyed by these signs of independence, Adam got God to banish Lilith. After that, God—who at the time was exclusively male and thus tended to side with Adam—gave him another partner, Eve, hoping she'd be more docile.

That partnership worked for a while, but it too eventually failed. Strolling outside the Garden of Eden one day, the more subservient Eve met Lilith. Overcoming her initial fears, she gazed into Lilith's face and recognized her own likeness. The same thing happened to Lilith when she returned Eve's gaze. Before long, they had initiated a friendship with questions like "Who are you?" and "What is your story?" After many hours of talking, listening, and dreaming, they became one. A part cast out was reclaimed; an incomplete woman became whole. This new woman returned to the garden, ready to re-create it with God and with Adam.

This story, first told in 1974 by theologian Judith Plaskow and a team of women refashioning the creation myth from women's perspective, introduces the work of the sixth Jubilee ritual. In it, we draw on memory and poetic imagery to share our personal stories with one another, to reclaim others untold until now, and to challenge false or inaccurate ones. Crossing the Threshold, Hallowing, Freedom, Journey, and Inventory are all rituals born of the memory that once upon a time we knew captivity and bondage. We were Liliths, separated from our land, our people, ourselves. We were Eves too, expected to serve others who were our masters. Even if we rarely dwell on them, we carry memories both of chains and coercion and of re-creation and new life.

Similar memories reside at the core of Jubilee spirituality. The reminder repeated throughout Leviticus 25—in verses 38, 42, and 55—"I your God brought you out of the land of Egypt, to give you the land of Canaan," is the refrain to the archetypal biblical song of captivity and release that grounds Jubilee teaching. The captivity ended when a gracious and powerful divinity said, "Come forth," and accompanied a once-enslaved people on a long, desert journey. In time, those Chosen People crossed the threshold into a land flowing with milk and honey. They exchanged Egypt for Canaan, and in doing so recognized they

EXERCISE 1

Memories of Story

1. Did you keep a diary as a girl? If so, what do you remember about keeping it?
2. Have you ever kept an adult journal? If so, when? For how long?
3. Have you used other forms besides writing for storying memories? If so, what are these forms?
4. Can you pinpoint a particular time you became interested in stories of women, especially stories of women's entire lives, not only our romances with men? If so, do you recall what sparked this interest?
5. Are there any stories of women you learned only in later adult life that have become important to you, sto-

possessed a story they had to preserve. Throughout the ancient biblical record, even in books other than Leviticus, the commandment recurs: "Remember. You must remember."

But the story demands more than simple remembering. We must record and tell our stories too, because they reveal meaning, origin, and destiny. The Book of Exodus carries the instruction that remembering and telling are only the first part of a ritual that culminates in the revelation that throughout our lives, a sacred Presence surrounds and guides us. As the next generation asks why our story is important—

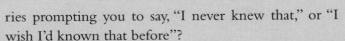

ries prompting you to say, "I never knew that," or "I wish I'd known that before"?

6. Are there any stories of women over 50—memoirs, biographies, films, family histories—that hold particular power for you? If so, what are they, and why do they engage you?

7. Thinking back, can you name an incident in your life when you might have identified with Lilith? Can you name an incident when you might have identified with Eve?

8. What is an "Egypt" in your life story? What is a "Canaan"?

9. Now turn the question around. Is there any sense in which "Canaan" is your place of slavery and "Egypt" your place of freedom?

"What does this mean?"—we must be ready to answer with the wisdom of our own interpretations, even as the ancient Hebrews were ready to answer with theirs: "By strength of hand the Lord brought us out of the house of slavery" (Exodus 13:15). We owe such storytelling not only to our children but to each other, especially to women reluctant to cross into Jubilee Time, for whom our stories may be an inspiration. We owe it to women of the past, those able to smuggle out fragments of life-telling from that far country, and those who had neither form nor forum for doing so. We owe it to ourselves. It is time to take up the ritual of memory, story, and witness, beginning with Exercise 1.

REMINISCENCE

Prior to 1963, experts on aging considered it somewhat unhealthy if an older person frequently recited tales beginning, "When I was a young woman . . ." or "When I was your age . . ." Too much reminiscence was believed to signal a dangerous preoccupation with happier times, even a refusal to live in the present.

But in 1963, Robert Butler, later the founder of the U.S. National Institute on Aging, published what turned out to be a landmark paper. In it, he presented clinical evidence interpreting elders' reminiscence in the most positive terms. He'd found that reminiscence wasn't regression, dependency, or denial, as too many thought then, and too many think still. Rather, it was a normal developmental task of life's second half.

Rose Dobrof, then a young woman beginning a long career with older people, remembers the impact of Butler's paper. Describing herself as "a very junior social worker" at a residence for the aging in the Bronx, she recalled being taught that living in the past was a pathology, a regression to childhood dependency, a denial of time's passage, even evidence of a damaged intellect—the kind of stereotyping I lamented in our third ritual.

"But then," she reports, "the Butler paper came out and was read and talked about, and our world changed." Reminiscence, or Life Review as it came to be called, "was the ground on which the old waged the struggle for integrity." Drawing on memory, older people were now encouraged to incorporate the past into their present lives, to regret it if need be, to look at it reflectively, and to try to understand it.

Butler went on to write a classic on aging, *Why Survive? Being Old in America,* which won a Pulitzer Prize in 1975. In an extended passage on the Life Review, he validated memory and story, and invited people to reminisce, encouraging oral history and promoting processes such as taped interviews. As examples, he cited the great memoirs composed in old age, "which not only provided fascinating accounts of unusual and gifted people but [were] of great historical value."

What Butler didn't say about those great historical memoirs was something that's become evident in the decades since: almost all recount the lives of men. Until well into the last part of this century, we have had few stories of women extending beyond the period of meeting a man, courtship, and marriage. We have fewer still recounting the second half of women's lives. As late as 1988, the year she published *Writing a Woman's Life,* Carolyn Heilbrun reminded us that the stories of women who didn't make men the center of their lives continue to strike us as unusual. We have few models of life-telling, or of the kinds of lives we want to live as older women.

GETTING OUT THE STORIES

This situation is finally changing, and women elders are in the lead. I've already mentioned Florida Scott-Maxwell's *The Measure of My Days,* written in her eighties, and May Sarton's many journals—including *Journal of a Solitude,* written when she was 60; *At Seventy;* and *Encore: A Journal of the Eightieth Year.* Novelist and critic Doris Grumbach is a more recent entry, with both *Coming Into the End Zone* and *Extra Innings*—playful metaphors we all might use as openings into our own stories.

Coming Into the End Zone begins on Grumbach's seventieth birthday, and she uses words like *terrible, despised,* and *disastrous* to describe her feelings about the passage into her eighth decade. A year later, her memoir ends. Once again, it is July twelfth, but this time she writes,

> No longer am I burdened by the weight of my years. My new age today, a year later, does not worry me. Alone for most of the day, until the promise of dinner with friends tonight, I went for a swim in the cove. . . . Nor is this day as painful as I thought it might be. I seem not to have grown older in the year, but more content with whatever age it is I am.

Similar shifts happen in our lives, and a journal gives us the opportunity to record ourselves in different frames of mind and states of soul from one year to the next. Journal entries testify that there are no foregone conclusions and that new chapters are always possible in the chronicles of our lives.

Having Our Say: The Delany Sisters' First 100 Years zoomed to the bestseller list as soon as it was published in 1993. In it, Sadie Delany, 103, and her younger sister Bessie, 101, tell their own story and that of their family, beginning with their father's birth into slavery in 1858 and his dance through the master's house seven years later singing, "I'm free. I'm free. I'm free." With artistry, sharp, clear memory, and a great deal of humor, the sisters describe singular personal and professional achievements— Bessie as only the second black woman licensed to practice dentistry in New York State, Sadie as the first to teach domestic science in the city's high schools. The book concludes with a rich legacy for women of age, as Bessie Delany confides, "I'll tell you a little secret. I'm starting to get optimistic."

Other significant stories that are finally coming to light center on painful memories hidden for decades. Prominent among these are accounts by Korean "comfort women" in their late sixties and seventies, who've finally revealed how they were kidnapped, forced into prostitution, and raped by Japanese forces during World War II. Moved by their determination, a Task Force on Filipino Comfort Women now exists and has already released a book on war crimes against Asian women. In a parallel to the Eve-Lilith conversations, Korean women from both the north and the south have been meeting with Japanese women in places such as Osaka and Tokyo to discuss *jungshindae,* as the comfort women issue is called. Together they're exploring its relation to world peace as well as to the reunification of Korea.

To focus on the work of older women's storytelling, Joyce Cupps gave birth to *Encore* in 1992. *Encore* is a grass-roots magazine celebrating the return of the Crone. I've spoken with 54-year-old Joyce several times since then, and each time felt her enthusiasm as she says things like, "The Crone is back! After centuries of rejection, the Crone has returned." She believes in the need to celebrate our lives as wise women, spiritual guides, healers, protectors of the young, and companions to the sick and dying—all roles associated with the Crone of ancient times. She supports the need of older women to tell our stories by publishing many of them in *Encore.*

Arisa, 54, introduces hers, "The Grandmother Archetype," with "I'm a maverick in the world, knocking about on my own, doing my 'priestess thing' wherever the Goddess sends me. I feel very wild inside, and this lifestyle suits me." Faye, an 87-year-old active musician, sums up her memories by writing, "From age fifty until now in my eighties, music has created new friends for me, kept me busy, uplifted my spirit and kept me happy." And Viola, born in 1903, proclaims, "On January 25, 1993, I became a ninety-year-old Crone! The delights of being ninety are: I am still learning; I am not worrying about 'what they say' about me; I am still wondering."

As I have traveled throughout North America leading Jubilee Time retreats, I have been struck by the impulse now urging large numbers of Jubilee women to tell our stories.

EXERCISE 2

Memoirs: Beginnings and Endings

A memoir is an account or autobiographical sketch of someone's personal experiences. We've just read some passages from Jubilee women's memoirs. This exercise invites you to join in this work and to use either prose or poetry as your form.

1. If you were to write the memoir of your life as a Jubilee woman, what might be your opening sentence or first line of verse?
2. What might be your closing sentence or last line of verse?

Writing is usually the preferred form, and I rarely lead an event without the women present talking about writing groups they belong to, or wanting to learn about writing practice. In Chicago, Peg, 60, asked me for resources that might help her do this (I recommended Natalie Goldberg's *Writing Down the Bones,* Christina Baldwin's *Life's Companion: Journal Writing as a Spiritual Quest,* and Gail Ranadive's *Writing Re-Creatively: A Spiritual Quest for Women*); in Kingston, Ontario, the high point of the retreat came when women took time to write and then share their memoirs; and in Grand Rapids, Michigan, when I asked her to fill out

3. What major incidents or themes would you include between the beginning and the end of your memoir? If each were to be a chapter in a book, how would you title the chapters?

4. Go ahead and write your responses. For a starter, limit yourself to three or four pages or to a period of fifteen minutes, where you don't lift your pen or worry about grammar, punctuation, or spelling.

5. If you're in a group, read what you've written to one another and listen without judgment or criticism. Think about sending your memoir to Joyce Cupps, Editor, *Encore Magazine,* 604 Pringle Avenue, Suite 91, Galt, CA 95632.

a questionnaire, Linda sent her response in the mail two weeks later, explaining:

> I'm just back from Florida and caring for my mother who has fallen and broken a hip. By the time I returned there was very little time to attend to your questions so I decided to use them this morning as part of my writing practice.
>
> Since the rules of writing practice allow (no, command) that you not lift your hand from the paper and refrain from crossing out or worrying about grammar and punctuation, it may seem these responses aren't thoughtfully written. But I did want to respond to you, and in this form: spirituality and the second half of life have been and continue to be conscious and crucial preoccupations for me.

Then she proceeded to confirm the power of writing practice with the following response.

> The best thing about growing older (I am now 54) is that I'm finding more and more of myself as time goes on. Starting 6 weeks before my 49th birthday, I have been on an active search to find out who I am, what I think, feel, like, want to do, and even eat. For some of that time I have been concerned that there really wasn't any real "I" in there—wherever *there* is—but mostly, despite the confusion, periods of doubt and insecurity, I recognize that the flaws and limitations I'd tried so hard to get rid of during earlier times were re-

ally part of me. The whole second half of life is turning out to be a grand adventure. (See Exercise 2.)

EXTENDING THE FORMS

Although we're all people of memory, not all of us need to be writers; we may not even be drawn to literary forms. When Martha, who is a historian, said to Mary, her 66-year-old mother, "I need to talk with you about your life story," she knew it wasn't Mary's style to write it, so she gave her a tape recorder. In the year since, Mary has become delighted with this opportunity, "grabbed hold of it," in her daughter's words, and in reflecting aloud into the microphone discovered within herself unasked questions, particularly about her religion, and liberating experiences, especially in her life as a woman who birthed twenty children. "These are gems I'd taken for granted," she says, "but the recorder has opened my eyes and my heart to the life I've led."

In the decades since the Life Review was introduced, it's become clear that we need not always use narrative, nor even verbal patterns, to story memories. We may even feel conscious resistance to reminiscing, recognizing that the work of memory is neither an easy nor a sentimental task. One British study, for example, found elders holding four conscious attitudes toward reminiscing. There were those who found it significant and positive; those who reminisced but remained unsatisfied; those who saw no point in looking back; and those who not only didn't like it, but found it painful.

That's led me to look for forms other than narrative writing. I came across two of them in studying the work of Kathleen Woodward, a gifted scholar who excels in interpreting the relations between later life and world literature, including Proust's *Remembrance of Things Past,* Virginia Woolf's *The Years,* and Eva Figes's *Waking.* Even so, Woodward maintains there are alternatives to narrative form that might fit some people better. She says some of us do the psychic work of reminiscence through *action in the world.* As I interpret this, it means that having had positive experiences of caring adults when we were children, for example, we may actively advocate generously funded day-care centers today. Having emigrated to the United States and becoming U.S. citizens, we may work to change immigration policies toward illegal aliens. Coming out as lesbians earlier in our lives, we may now put our energies into organizing older lesbians, or—as Rita, 67, is doing—creating group homes and living arrangements for homosexual women. Hungry for a deeper spiritual life, we may decide to enter the ministry. Such actions in the world incarnate our reminiscence.

An alternative possibility is *mythicizing* our pasts rather than making explicit sense of them, finding symbols to represent our memories rather than offering straightforward, sequential accounts. Janet Bloom gives a striking description of how this works by telling the story of "Minerva's Doll."

Director of a writing group at a New York City senior center, Bloom instructed her students: "Choose an important object from home and describe it for the rest of us. Bring it in to our meetings if you'd like." In the group's first session, Minerva Rios described a beloved doll; in later sessions, she brought the doll itself so that everyone might see it.

The doll was of the kind familiar and important in Puerto Rican culture. Once it had been very beautiful; now its head was coming apart. Janet Bloom took down Minerva's words exactly, but did so in verse, rather than in paragraphs, in order to illuminate their poetic force and capture Minerva's vocal rhythms.

> Oh! how I remember my doll, dressed like a Spanish lady
> sitting in the middle of my bed
> with her elegant hair combed
> and black lace veil down to her waist
> and her satin and black lace dress.
> She looked so beautiful adorning my bed.
>
> Now I only look for a way by which I can find a new
> head or fix the one she already has.

Listening to Minerva and recording what she was saying about the doll over several weeks, Bloom eventually realized the doll symbolized Minerva herself. As the sessions continued it became evident that Minerva was facing a cataract operation and possible blindness, even death. Minerva never connected herself consciously with the crumbling face of the doll. But in a nonconscious way, she used the doll as a vehicle to tell a critical part of her story. The doll became a surrogate, enabling her to trust her story to Bloom and the group, and to give them both the internal reminiscence and the hope she was carrying as she compared her own "crumbling" face to the doll's.

Long after these sessions ended, Bloom reflected on how Minerva had used the vehicle of the doll to name death as well as parts of her story too difficult to deal with directly. She said that if you develop very careful listening, you also develop an

---

Symbols of Ourselves

In this exercise we choose something in our home we identify with. If we trust the process, we may discover hidden facets of our stories and our lives.

Begin by attending to your breath. Inhale and exhale at least ten times, choosing as a mantra the word *story* or the word *memory*. When you are calm and quiet, respond to the following.

1. Choose a very familiar and important object in your home and describe it. Draw or sketch the object. If

---

intuition for those instances when a person can live best through a symbol. Such a form of reminiscence can protect our stories from breakage or manipulation.

I've found Exercise 3 particularly revealing personally, and its connection with my Jubilee years profound. When I did it, the object I chose was my spinet piano. When I retired from the convent over twenty years ago, my mother gave me the piano—like her, I'm a lifelong musician. When I first did the exercise, I asked the piano to speak and found it crying. I'd ignored it too often, been too busy to play it. It acted as a Jubilee symbol by beckoning me to return to my music, to reincorporate it into my story, and to celebrate my own Sabbath of Sabbaths.

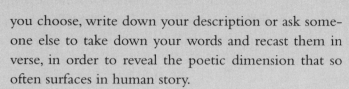

you choose, write down your description or ask someone else to take down your words and recast them in
verse, in order to reveal the poetic dimension that so
often surfaces in human story.

2. When did the object enter your life? If it were to have a
    voice and tell its story, what would it say about your re-
    lationship with it? Listen and copy down what it says.

3. Who are some of the people in your life associated
    with this object? How are they connected to it?

4. In what ways has the object been a source of freedom
    for you? Are there ways it's been a constraint?

5. In what ways is the object like you?

6. In what ways is it different?

7. In what ways do you regularly care for the object?

The two story avenues of action in the world and mythicizing through symbol can come together in our later years as
we feel impulses to remember and put to rest parts of our stories we regret or—the religious word is apt—repent. Just as the
first Jubilee people include in their story the armed, bloody
takeover of another people's land, recalled in the Book of
Joshua, so we and our people regularly carry memories of
troubling, even violent acts too. Confession and repentance—
physical or symbolic—are good for the soul.

So is asking forgiveness. It may be as complex a part of our
story as lobbying for Native American causes as a way of re-
penting the federal government's takeovers of native peoples'

land and the resulting trails of tears, or selling a second house—as Peggy, 53, and her husband did—because we believe that is a way to remember the poor in our midst. It may be as simple as a personal phone call, a hug, or a greeting card sent to thaw a frozen silence. I recall feeling uneasy before an upcoming meeting recently, because I knew I'd be working with a woman whose application I had once turned down when I was doing personnel work; it had been years since I'd seen her. We'd hit it off when we first met, and though I wasn't ultimately responsible, I'd always felt some guilt for not contacting her to express my regret.

She had ambivalent feelings too. But the day of the meeting, those feelings were dissipated for both of us. Catching each other's glance immediately as the group gathered, we moved toward each other, saying nothing as we did. Instead we embraced with a hug that was far more than perfunctory. Our embrace was forgiveness gesture enough, a symbolic embrace that said far more than any words would have done.

THE STORYTELLER'S VOCATION

Throughout our lives we have told stories; this is not an experience new to Jubilee Time. Still, we now find one major difference. As elders, telling stories is more than something occasional; it's a Jubilee vocation, a calling. Made "three stories tall" by our Jubilarian status, we link members of several generations to their own stories, as well as to those of their ancestors. We also take on the protestant's role of questioning false stories, and the wise woman's role of recasting ancient ones. This ritual anoints us as preservers, challengers, and interpreters.

PRESERVERS

As family elders, we preserve ancestors' stories for the next generation. We also preserve parts of children's or younger persons' individual stories, holding in escrow the early years unavailable to them before they became self-conscious: "Tell me about when I was little." No photo album or videotape can compete with the emotional impact of a memory about him- or herself passed on to a child by a beloved elder.

To members of our own generation, especially friends or siblings, we are life preservers too, reminders of stands taken, hesitations overcome, games lost. In a discussion for Jubilee women just last month, Dulcie—my best friend of forty-five years—reminded me of our experience discovering Bach's *Mass in b minor* in the 1950s and Brahms's *German Requiem* in the 1960s, music that's seen both of us through deaths in our families. As best friends do, she regularly reminds me of experiences I've forgotten, as for example when I stood up to an administrator who had tried to bully me into rejecting a student, or when I initially turned down a teaching assignment in Boston that ended up changing my life.

Sitting near us, two sisters, both in their seventies, nodded, eager to contribute their experiences. Rachel turned to address Becky. "You've held all my most precious secrets as far back as I can remember. You know every nuance of my love life, my politics. You know I'm a pushover for every troubled kid in the neighborhood." As her eyes filled with tears she declared to the rest of us, "Becky's the custodian—the guardian—of my memories."

CHALLENGERS

Some Jubilee Time stories are meant to be challenged as well. Eileen, now approaching her forty-ninth birthday, recently taught a group of us one way to do that. I'd asked the participants to bring in a favorite fairy tale from childhood so we might discover what it revealed both about our early years and about the women we are now. A high-school teacher of young women, Eileen lis-

---

EXERCISE 4

Pauses for Storytelling

Pause here to examine the preserver and challenger roles in your own life story.

Part 1: Preserving
1. Name at least three people who carry stories from your life for you. Who preserves stories of your childhood? Who regularly reminds you of pieces of your story you may have forgotten?
2. What's at least one story about yourself you associate with each of these storytellers?
3. Have you ever told them what this means to you?

tened as each of us shared our choices. Mine was "The Six Swans" from the Brothers Grimm; Thecla, sitting next to me, in her late forties and still seeking Mr. Right, revealed that she continued to hold on to the hope embodied in "Cinderella."

Then Eileen spoke up, not about her own story, but about some of the harmful effects fairy tales can have. They can teach, for example, that "stepmother" equals "person without care for little children." They can lead to believing all life's discomfort ends once the glass slipper fits. They can foster the assumption that witches are evil, rather than embodiments of mystical wisdom, magic, and enchantment.

4. Who are some of the people for whom you carry stories? How?

Part 2: Challenging
1. What are some fairy tales—if any—you revered in childhood?
2. Is there anything in them you want to challenge now?
3. What, if anything, in your own story do you want to challenge—something you were once told, but have learned to recognize as untrue?
4. What are some family stories—of denial or untruth—you need to challenge? How might you do so?
5. Recall some of the people who've taught you to challenge stories. How did they do that?

I don't know if it's directly traceable to fairy tales, which I loved as a child, but I do know the stepmother image had a strong negative impact on me. My grandmother was a marvelous storyteller, and I loved going to her house because she always seemed to know new ones. But somewhere around my seventh birthday, a relative cruelly said to me, "You know she's not your *real* grandmother, don't you? She's only your *step*-grandmother." He was referring to my grandfather's remarriage, and to my "real" grandmother's early death.

I regret it took me decades to challenge his false teaching. Although Bammy continued to be a warm source of love, I began to believe she wasn't quite what a grandmother should be. She wasn't my mother's mother; she was her stepmother. Then some years ago, planning to take part in a ritual on aging, I learned each of us was to bring a memento of an older woman who'd had a strong impact on our lives. I often wear my grandmother's antique watch; I inherited it when she died in 1973. I remember carefully choosing it as my memento for the ritual because when I got there I wanted to say something. When my turn came, I held up the watch and told the other women it had belonged to a woman who—contrary to the story I'd once believed—was my *real* grandmother. She was the only grandmother I knew, and she gave me the gift of unconditional love. (See Exercise 4.)

INTERPRETERS

Having remembered and told our stories, the crucial task of later life becomes interpreting them, and on occasion—as with my grandmother story—reinterpreting them. Teaching other women to pick out and follow the thread of interpretation, I've discovered they pluck it from the story in three ways: through naming, through reclaiming, and through using poetic imagery.

Naming

I became sensitive to naming in older women's stories when I met Jeanne, who has since become a close friend. "What's your whole name?" I asked her early on. She smiled enigmatically, then said, "That's not so easy, Maria. Actually, from one perspective it's Norma Jane Grant Allen D'Acosta."

Jeanne?

She explained.

Born into the Grant family and named Norma Jane, she'd never used the Norma and never liked the Jane. So in high school she dropped the first and changed the second, becoming Jean to everyone who met her, which evolved into Jeanne. Her first marriage, to Ted Allen, ended in divorce, but by then her daughter had been born and given his name. So she too stayed with Allen. Then she remarried and became D'Acosta, although her daughter didn't. After her second divorce she went back to Grant. At 52, she's finally become Jeanne Grant.

From hearing Jeanne's story, I've learned to do a complete naming go-around during a workshop or seminar. When I work with Jubilee women who will be probing story in their lives, I no longer say, "Please introduce yourself by telling us your name." As I indicated in the last chapter, I now ask women to think for a few moments about every name they've ever had, recall the associations each name has for them, and remember personal stories these various names evoke. Then, when they introduce themselves, I ask them to tell the rest of us their *entire* name and, should they want, any connections they've made. As they do, memories surface and tales tumble forth.

Sometimes, one woman's naming provokes another woman's recollections. Recently, for example, when we came to Mary, 58, she said, "I'm Mary Elizabeth Ann Schmidt Callan. Even though I go by Mary, Mary Elizabeth is the important name; it was my mother's and my grandmother's too.

"The older I get, the more it means to me to have this as a tie to those two women," she continued, "especially to my grandmother, because my children don't remember her. The name's my way of connecting her story to theirs."

Later in the circle, Carole, 59, picked up on this. Her first name was Audrey but she'd never used it, preferring her second name, Carole, instead. But then she told us, "Mary reminded me that I'm a Mary Elizabeth too—I'm a Catholic and I took that as my confirmation name. I remember we were allowed only one, but I wanted the double name for myself because it was also my grandmother's. Confirmation day was the first time the nun preparing me realized I was asking for two names. During the ceremony, I was on my way up to the bishop when Sister read the card I was to hand him and saw I'd written two names. "You can't ask for two," she whispered to me, but I answered, "Well, if he doesn't like it, he can confirm me with only one."

She got both names. But the incident confirmed something else. "Even then, at 12," she admitted, "I was a rebel."

This unexpected conversation about grandmothers touched Pam, 54, who quietly said, "I'd like to tell you all something." When we turned to her, she began slowly, reflectively. "We've been talking about mothers and grandmothers and that's set me thinking. My mother and my grandmother were very strong women, and I've never felt myself like them—I'm really a hesitant person."

Then, as if connecting to something inside herself for the first time, she went on. "Last September, at one-thirty in the morning, I had a call from a hospital in the Caribbean. My sister had survived a near-drowning, but her husband hadn't. For the first time in my life I was the central figure in my family, doing the things the strong ones had always done—arranging for the body to be brought back, meeting my sister, contacting my brother-in-law's family, preparing for his burial. I know myself differently now. When the time in my life came for needing their strength, those two women passed it on to me."

Reclaiming

We have already followed the thread of reclaiming by encountering Eve and Lilith earlier in this chapter, and Inanna and Erishkegal in the Journeys ritual, finding they model aspects of ourselves that sometimes lie dormant within us. Many of these female figures emerge from religious tradition, and in reclaiming them, we also reinterpret the tradition. Among them are several older-younger pairs, including Elizabeth and Mary, Naomi and Ruth, and Sarah and Hagar.

Elizabeth and Mary are usually celebrated—particularly in painting—as the mothers of John the Baptist and Jesus. But as contemporary women reclaiming them, we do better to focus on a major element in their identities only peripherally related to their sons: their relation to each other. The first chapter of Luke describes Mary's reaction when she learned she was pregnant with the baby who would be called Jesus: she immediately rushed across the countryside to seek out her older cousin Elizabeth. Elizabeth was the mature, wise woman to whom the younger instinctively turned for succor and comfort. As she approached Elizabeth, Mary traveled slowly, up a hill, unsure of hope, advice, or consolation. But when Elizabeth heard Mary's voice calling her name, and stepped outside her house, she knew the younger woman's story intuitively, directly, because life had taught her to listen. She knew from the tremors in Mary's voice that she was alone and frightened, pregnant and unmarried. She handed over her knowing that as a gift. When she did, Mary leaned on her, felt her weariness leave, and soared into the poem known as the *Magnificat.* "My soul is big with God," Mary sang, "and my spirit rejoices in the One who is doing great things in me."

Found in the Bible's Book of Ruth, the tale of Naomi and her daughter-in-law Ruth is another such story. Often presented as a romance between Ruth and the rich landowner, Boaz, we can reclaim it even more powerfully by interpreting it as a story of love between an older and a younger woman.

The story begins with the older, widowed Naomi deciding to journey back to her home in Bethlehem, her "Canaan," after losing not only her husband but her two sons to death. Ruth, her daughter-in-law, insists on accompanying her. In her insistence, Ruth gives the world one of its most treasured testimonies of human love, expressed not between a woman and a man, but between two women. Binding herself forever to the older woman, Ruth vows to Naomi,

> Do not press me to leave you
> or to turn back from following you!
> Where you go, I will go;
> Where you lodge, I will lodge;
> your people shall be my people,
> and your God my God.

Where you die, I will die—
there will I be buried.

For her part, Naomi teaches Ruth how to gather food, how to seduce Boaz, how to find economic security. After Ruth's remarriage and the birth of her child, the story ends as it began, focusing not on Ruth but on the elder Naomi. The story concludes, "Then Naomi took the child and laid him in her bosom and became his nurse," and with the women of the neighborhood singing in celebration, "A son has been born to Naomi!"

I've worked with women to reclaim a third pair too: Hagar and Sarah. In Jewish and Christian lore, Sarah is the woman of age, wife of Abraham, and mother of his second-born son, Isaac. That child's birth came, however, only after the apparently barren Sarah's place was taken by Hagar, Abraham's Arab "concubine," who bore Ishmael. In Moslem lore, as I've learned from Christian-Jewish-Islamic conversations, Hagar is considered a true wife like Sarah, not a slave.

I begin one process for reclaiming them by showing a representation of George Segal's sculpture *Abraham's Farewell to Ishmael.* In it, Sarah stands in shadow and toward the back, presiding over the banishment the Bible reports she demanded. Isaac isn't present. But as Abraham embraces Ishmael, Hagar's face is already turned toward the journey into the desert.

After viewing this tableau in silence, I usually ask, "Where are you in this scene?" as a way of evoking parts of each woman's story. Some women identify with Sarah: "I'm a privileged woman, allowing the dismissal of a woman who doesn't fit my culture." Others identify with Hagar: "I'm a woman acting on her own power, refusing to accept a situation of

Exercise 5

On Doing Midrash

Midrash is a method of imaginatively interpreting biblical stories. This book, reinterpreting Jubilee for contemporary women, is a kind of midrash; so too is the Eve-Lilith story that opened this ritual. In this exercise, you are asked to reinterpret one of the three stories just described, and to connect it with your own.

1. What is a Mary-Elizabeth encounter in your life? When have you been Mary? When have you been Elizabeth?
2. Who is a Ruth for you? Who is a Naomi?
3. Where and when are you a Ruth?
4. Where and when are you a Naomi?
5. Reread the Sarah-Hagar story from the Bible (Genesis 16:1–21:21). Where and when have you been Sarah? Where and when have you been Hagar?
6. If you are alone, retell the story, either in writing—poetry or prose—or by drawing it so the women are not made into enemies.
7. If you are with others, retell the story together in whatever form you choose.

bondage." Still others interpret it as did Harriet, 64, who said, "I'm neither. Instead I'm standing in the scene as myself and shouting to both Sarah and Hagar, 'Don't be driven apart. It's only together that we can be free.'"

A second way to reclaim the story is to use it as the basis of a "living sculpture." Here, instead of talking about the story, we enact it. I ask women to form groups of four or five, and then go off on their own to reshape, refashion, and reinterpret the story with a depiction fitting women today. Perhaps they can avoid the separation, the banishment; perhaps not. They return with a variety of responses. Sometimes Hagar and Sarah link arms; sometimes Sarah is kneeling, asking Hagar's forgiveness; sometimes Abraham is left out of the picture; sometimes the two women separate regretfully. But whatever they do in response, women interpret the story of an older and younger woman for themselves by using their own bodies to tell it. (See Exercise 5.)

Poetic Imagery

"Do you have an image or a picture, a song or a book title that represents Jubilee Time in your life?" I asked that question in my original questionnaire; I continue to ask it today. I've learned from decades of teaching imaginative processes that if a person can enter the metaphoric world—often through poetic imagery—she can discover parts of her story inaccessible through more prosaic media.

Although a few women have said things like "I don't think in images" or even "Heavens, no!" most respond without hesitation, and many choose with care. One seventy-one-year-old, citing Shakespeare's sonnet about the "beauteous springs to yellow autumn turned," sent me back to pore over those verses with their poetic commentary on later life. Helen, 70, choosing the book title *When Gods Die,* said it gave her courage to let the fake self she was carrying around die and "to live a new life in the spirit." Mary, 71, chose the rolling sea at her doorstep, and explained, "With age, things are constantly in flux, just as the ocean is. Still, like me, they're grounded in something that goes on forever."

One image that continues to arrest me came from seventy-one-year-old Claudia, who responded, "For me, it's the book title *Surprised by Joy.* It reminds me of the experience I've had lately of sudden unexplained epiphanies, which sometimes last for days . . . feelings of joyful anticipation." I was so taken by her comment that I wanted to hear more. So some months after receiving her response, I phoned.

Her husband answered. When I told him who I was and why I was calling, he said, "I'm sorry, but I'm afraid you're too late. She died, suddenly, last January."

I think of that as a shining witness to Claudia's insight into her Jubilee Time. I believe her final unexplained epiphany was her death, and that she continues to be surprised by the Joy that beckoned her forth.

Other women use more extensive imagery. Sixty-five-year-old Mary Hoffman offered the following poem to me, saying, "This is my picture of the beauty of life, and old age's relinquishing this to some extent with the realization of death. But then the new thought comes: there is growth still and hope and beauty to look forward to always." Here is what she wrote.

I will not walk that way again.

The flower is dead,
dried on the vine.

It no longer unfurls for me
as I pass by,
like a daily greeting.

I cannot walk that way again.
There is no beauty to behold,
no life, no color.
The intrigue of the opening leaf
was what caught my heart.

I cannot walk that way again.
It is a sad way to walk.

To have a living thing
become just a memory . . .

Yet, if I do not go that way
I may miss the first sign,
a tiny green bud that heralds
new life,
the unfurling to come.

Perhaps I should go again . . .
to keep watch,
to wait for Hope.

Such poetry often erupts into song. The kind of song I have in mind is celebrated in a powerful creation myth from Down Under. Aboriginal people in Australia believe that during the time of their origins—what they call the Dreamtime—their ancestors scattered a trail of musical notes along the lines of their footprints, and these musical tracks became ways of re-membering. A song acted as both map and direction finder, and if you knew the song, you could find your way anywhere. The whole country could be imagined as a musical score. There wasn't a rock or creek or tree that hadn't been sung. You didn't dig or shape or hammer things into existence, you sang them. Songs lay all over the earth in patterns called Songlines that held wonderful stories just waiting for a creative, artistic person to sing them into life.

In this ritual, we are such troubadors, singing a new older woman into existence. This woman has survived many centuries of enforced silence and incomplete accounts. She is finally free to record her story. But she is also free to tell the stories and sing the songs of the "unnumbered women dead" memorialized in the anthem "Bread and Roses." She keeps faith with these women in recalling their stories, even as she bears witness to, remembers, and celebrates her own.

Seven

The Song of Gratitude

You shall have the trumpet sounded throughout all your land. For it is a jubilee; it shall be holy to you.

Lev. 25:9, 12

In 1955, at the beginning of her forty-ninth year, Anne Morrow Lindbergh wrote the now classic *Gift from the Sea*. Feeling the pressure of work, deadlines, and homemaking for a husband and five children, she took a cottage by the water, alone for a brief respite. Lying on the beach at night, solitary under the stars, and eating her breakfast in the dawn's quiet, she felt herself dwelling in an atmosphere of awe.

"It seemed to me, separated from my own species, that I was nearer to others," she wrote. She noticed the shy willet, the sandpiper, the pelican flapping slowly over her head, the old gull studying the horizon. As she did she felt gratitude well up within her.

Beauty of earth and sea and air meant more to me. I
was in harmony with it, melted into the universe, lost
in it, as one is lost in a canticle of praise swelling from
an unknown crowd in a cathedral. "Praise ye the Lord,
all ye fishes of the sea—all ye birds of the air—all ye
children of men—Praise ye the Lord!"

Her gathered years, her pause for solitude, and her receptivity
had escorted her into the ritual of Gratitude.

We have arrived at this point too, and are ready for the final ritual of Jubilee Time. Gathering our own years, and don-
ning the garment of receptivity, we turn to the work of
thanksgiving and praise, where we honor the gifts surrounding
us, dwell in the feelings of gratitude they evoke, and give those
feelings expression. Joining Jubilee women who have preceded
us, such as Anne Morrow Lindbergh, we add our voices to the
ongoing canticle of celebration.

With clarity and precision, the original biblical teaching
provides the genesis of this ritual. "After you have counted off
seven weeks of years so that you total forty-nine years, you
shall have the trumpet sounded loud; you shall have the trumpet sounded loud throughout all your land. And you shall hallow the fiftieth year because it is a jubilee; it shall be holy to
you." That fiftieth year ushers in new thresholds, Sabbath, and
liberation; journeys, inventory, and story. We have explored
these in the previous rituals.

But we have also explored the poetic, metaphoric, and
spiritual force of Jubilee. When we listen attentively to the
command to sound the trumpet, we find something else,
something deeper and more personal to us. "You shall have the
trumpet sounded throughout *all your land,* for *it* is a jubilee"

suggests that we ourselves are Jubilee land. The previous rituals have taught us that not only is our fiftieth year a jubilee, so is life's entire second half. And so this teaching becomes a guide for every day. It—your existence—is a jubilee. It shall be holy to you.

How, precisely, shall we be a jubilee? In ordinary practice throughout the world, a jubilee is a time set aside after a significant period of years for rejoicing, festivity, and thanksgiving. Although each of the earlier Jubilee rituals provides an occasion to sound the ram's horn or *yobel,* from which we get the word *jubilee,* this ritual provides Jubilee's sacramental center. We must become living embodiments of thanksgiving, praise, and gratitude, directing each of these beyond ourselves to the Source of all gifts. Our canticle is incomplete if it stops at *"Jubilate,"* which translates as "Give thanks and glory and praise." It must go on to *"Jubilate Deo"*—"Give thanks and glory and praise to God." Before the Mystery of Being itself, however we name that Mystery, we must give thanks and we must *be* thanks—or perish from ingratitude.

As a people, the Hebrews—ancient and modern—never forgot this. Even when captured by the conquering armies of Nebuchadnezzar, who exiled them to Babylon, even in the ghettoes and in the camps, they praised and gave thanks to their God, Yahweh. They created the biblical book called Psalms, where characteristic opening verses are:

I thank you, Yahweh, with all my heart; I sing praise to you before the gods. (Psalm 138)

I will give thanks to God with my whole heart; I will tell of all God's wonderful deeds. (Psalm 9)

I give thanks to you, Yahweh, for you are good, your love is everlasting. (Psalm 118)

As the centuries piled up, the Hebrews acted on the counsel of the Talmud that in every generation, at every Passover feast, at every weekly Sabbath, and during every seventh year, each would regard herself as though she (or he) had just emerged from Egypt, and in remembering, give thanks. Such is the store of gratitude on which this ritual draws.

EXERCISE 1

A Mantra for Every Day

As a prelude to the major work of this ritual, take a moment to acknowledge the gifts in everyday life. At the start of the day or at bedtime, pause to become centered and quiet. Attend to your breath, repeating the phrase "thank you" as you breathe in. Then repeat "thank you" as you breathe out. Next, inhale on the words "thank you" and hold for four seconds, as in "thank you—two—three—four." Then exhale for four seconds, as in "thank you—two—three—four."

Close your eyes, and when you have repeated the mantra several times, imagine the gifts of the day, those you expect or those you've received: gifts of mind, heart, body. Gifts of people, places, things. Supermarkets, stop signs, music. A mended hip; the ability to read.

AN INJURED ART

In slower, less shattered, and more overtly religious eras than ours, the natural connections among jubilee, gratitude, and the fullness of years were taken for granted. Poets and saints, mystics and dreamers regularly reminded us we were surrounded by gifts. Each day was a gift, each evening. Each breath, each rainfall, each person.

In contrast, our own century's intense search for a richer, renewed spirituality signifies a hunger for such awareness, too

Use the pattern of *see, feel,* and *express* to focus on the day's gifts.

1. As you think of the gifts in your daily life, which do you see first, either in your mind's eye or right there in front of you? Slowly, enumerate at least five of these.
2. What do you feel in response to these gifts? Tenderness, wonder, surprise, luck? Something else?
3. How might you express your gratitude for at least one of them during the day—through music, art, words, silent contemplation? Resolve to make such an expression at a particular time during the coming day, or right now, if you choose.
4. Conclude this exercise with a five-minute repetition of the mantra "thank you."

often left behind in the race toward modernization. Jubilee Time provides an opportunity to satisfy that hunger. So we ask ourselves how gratitude might reenter the world; how we might return to giving and receiving; how awe might reanimate our imaginations.

In this ritual we explore gratitude's rhythms as a way of responding to these questions. We apply the arts of hallowing, receptivity, and spiritual assessment learned in rituals previous to this one. The three steps that make up this final ritual—recognizing gifts, experiencing gratitude, and expressing thanksgiving—lead us to understand the relations between gratitude and evil, gratitude and dying, and gratitude and being. (See Exercise 1.)

STEP 1: RECOGNIZING GIFTS

We pause for this opening exercise because many of us fail to notice the universe of gifts in which we dwell. Such awareness often lies dormant, since commodity exchanges and business relations have squeezed the meaning out of the word *gift*. Unlike advertising and sales promotions that offer "free" gifts—"Bank with us and we'll give you a toaster"; "Listen to our two-hour sales pitch and tonight's five-course dinner is on us"—real gifts are free by definition. Genuine gifts are unearned and impose no debt on the receiver. Unless freely and unconditionally given, they aren't gifts at all.

Even if we understand the true meaning of gifts and maintain a deep awareness of them, however, we may lack a contemplative context in which to appreciate them. The ability to recognize life's gifts arises from what Buddhists call "mindfulness." The ritual of Gratitude exacts a disposition to live in the present *attentively*, in order to see with the Awakened Eye of thanksgiving.

Thich Nhat Hanh, the great Buddhist teacher of mindfulness, tells of asking some children, "What is the purpose of eating breakfast?" One child answers that it's to get energy for the day, but another says the purpose of eating breakfast is eating breakfast. Commenting on the exchanges, Nhat Hanh says he thinks the second child is more correct. Unless we know how to be where we are and do what we're doing, we miss the gift of the moment. We dwell in either the past or the future, but not in the present.

We can learn to develop such presence and incorporate a continuing disposition of gratitude into our lives at any age. Nevertheless, we're more likely to do so in our Jubilee years as our pace slows, our ambition wanes, and our values undergo transformation. Leading retreats in Jubilee spirituality, I've recently discovered a powerful practice to enable this process.

Over the past year, when I'm asked what equipment I'll need for my sessions (microphone, overhead projector, VCR, slide projector, etc.) I have added one new item—a handbell. Sometimes a person brings one from a bell choir; sometimes it's a small glass bell; at other times it's a schoolyard bell recalling the routines of childhood. On occasion I've brought my own, a brass antique with a haunting overtone that I picked up in London's Portobello Road market last year for seven pounds.

When I arrive at the retreat, I ask for a volunteer who agrees to act as community bell ringer, and over longer retreats, I ask for several volunteers. When the retreat begins, I draw attention to the bell ringer, telling the participants that she will sound it every half hour during our time together. When she does, whether someone's speaking or we're doing an exercise or eating a meal or reapplying our lipstick, we agree to pause silently for no less than twenty-five or thirty seconds and no more than a minute. I suggest people let the silence cloak them when those moments arrive, so they may be mindful, still, and attentive to their breathing. So they may be grateful. I suggest they choose a mantra but if not, simply close their eyes.

Invariably, the bell turns out to be the centerpiece of the retreat. Even without my suggesting it, people tell me they've already begun thinking about what signal they'll choose in their own home to continue the practice once the retreat is over. If I have a conversation with retreatants in subsequent weeks or months, they tell me how they've incorporated this reminder into their daily life. Often, they choose a bell too: it's a more accessible *yobel* than the harder-to-find ram's horn. But

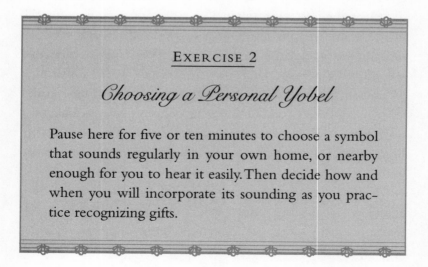

EXERCISE 2

Choosing a Personal Yobel

Pause here for five or ten minutes to choose a symbol that sounds regularly in your own home, or nearby enough for you to hear it easily. Then decide how and when you will incorporate its sounding as you practice recognizing gifts.

others choose the telephone's ring, the chime of a clock, or the ever-present sirens of city traffic. To deepen the silence, they may choose a mantra too, and it often turns out to be the one we recited earlier: "thank you." (See Exercise 2.)

STEP 2: THE RESPONSE OF GRATITUDE

Although I didn't ask questions about gifts directly, women I interviewed or who responded to my questionnaire spontaneously named the presence of gifts as one of the great accompaniments to the second half of life. As we saw during the ritual of Inventory—a sister to Gratitude—a few mentioned possessions and material security, but the great majority cited realities that couldn't be purchased. Marie, 72, commented, "You can't buy happiness because the best things in life really are free. When I think about my reaction to that, I realize I'm usually stumbling over my ever-present gratitude—it's never far from my soul." Where Maude, 62, talked about the gift of good health, 55-year-old Anne made the thoughtful comment, "Not only has health been a gift; for me, illness has been too. I've even learned to appreciate what pain has taught me." Ethel, 67, said, "I enjoy every day. I was sickly as a child, but God has been good and I feel grateful for what I've come through with His help."

Eighty-four-year-old Ruth exclaimed, "So many benefits, I can hardly count them all!" but then she tried, beginning with, "The best gift in age is my broadened perspective. I see today's events in a wider focus, and as part of new and ever more mellow relationships." When I asked the direct question "How do you feel about growing older?" women regularly used the

Reactivating Gratitude Through a Private Retreat

One way to evoke and enhance gratitude as a continuing ritual in our personal Jubilee Time is to set apart a three-day period in which you will heed and respond to the gifts of nature. Imitating Anne Morrow Lindbergh's observations of the living beings around her—willet, sandpiper, pelican, gull, beauty of earth and sea and air—decide now, at the beginning of this exercise, that over the next seventy-two hours, you will use your journal to enumerate similar gifts of nature.

Plan not only to name them, but to add two or three descriptive phrases for each gift (for example, ". . . the sandpiper, running in little unfrightened steps down the shining beach rim ahead of me" or ". . . the strong green weed, triumphantly emerging through crevices of concrete and proclaiming, 'Here is new life.' "). You may want to

phrase "I feel grateful," with blessing a recurring motif. "It's a blessing that comes with each day," said Muffy, 51. "Growing older is a blessing," said Juanita, 67, adding, "And that includes the solitary life I'm now enjoying after rearing five children." Like Berta, 65, they responded to the gifts of their later years as

record your observations through drawing, sketching, or taking photographs of each gift.

To make this private retreat, take the following steps:

1. Decide ahead that at least three times each day over the next three days, during morning, afternoon, and evening, you will note down a gift of nature whose path you cross: a living being such as a bird, fish, cat, dog; a flower, vegetable, plot of earth, tree; a stone, a fiber of cloth, a mineral in the form of gem or jewel.
2. Now choose the exact times when you will do this.
3. Next choose how long each session will be—five minutes, fifteen minutes, thirty minutes.
4. Prepare your materials: journal, sketch pad, camera.
5. Set an alarm for the starting time of the first session, and plan to reset it subsequently for each period chosen over the three days.

Alternate or additional option: this exercise may be done in preparation for or during a group session where a number of women celebrate nature's gifts together in a communal retreat.

freely bestowed. "I have strength of character," Berta wrote, "but I didn't earn it. It was given to me in my creation."

At first, comments such as these might seem to repeat earlier ritual work of counting up and counting off. But there's a difference, more accurately a completion, when we enter Gratitude. In Inventory, we count up and count off to illuminate personal identity; in Gratitude, we realize that achieving identity or becoming ourselves is more than a private task and involves the world around us. Selfhood demands that we be open to "otherness"—to everything beyond ourselves—and, most critically, to *the* Other.

As a prerequisite to such openness, gratitude requires humility. If our focus is always on ourselves, we aren't able to recognize people and things outside us as sources of gifts, and we're certainly not likely to be surprised by wonder. But if we cultivate gratitude, we discover it liberates us from egotism and selfishness and from assuming we are the apex of creation. Free of the false notion that we possess others—and the Other—we are able to praise and give thanks.

"Gratitude is the virtue that all devout women and men share," writes philosopher Louis Dupre. "The Buddhist as well as the Benedictine monk *thanks* all day long independent of personal mood or feeling. The monk thanks because it is morning, noon, or evening. At the end of the day, monks sing their thanks for whatever the day has brought—pleasure, boredom or pain. . . . Every day is Godgiven, and as such, good." (See Exercise 3.)

Step 3: Thanksgiving

It is one thing to recognize the gifts in our life. It is an additional thing to feel gratitude for them. But to complete the ritual, we must cultivate practices of thanksgiving that declare and communicate our gratitude. We must join the monks in thanking—not just thinking—all day.

Thanksgiving, especially to God or to the Universe of Being, is gratitude's more active partner, its *expression*. It is also a naturally spiritual act. In many countries, for example in the United States and in Canada on their respective Thanksgiving Days, thanksgiving takes the form of a solemn public celebration, where people often use the language of prayer to give thanks for divine benefits. On these occasions, what specifies us as human communities is that we shout our "Praise be" and "Glory be" together in the centers of our towns and cities with song, ceremony, and parade.

But we also need to express thanks personally and privately. Many women who've spoken to me of thanksgiving take it on as a regular, daily practice, as familiar as brushing their teeth or talking with their children on the phone. If they don't, as 54-year-old Regina says, "We run and keep too busy, missing the inner movement toward Jubilee." Three of the most natural times for giving thanks are on awakening, just before falling asleep, and when granted the blessing of food.

Barbara, 63, gives thanks by reciting the Twenty-third Psalm every morning on waking: "The Lord is my shepherd, I shall not want / He makes me lie down in green pastures / He leads me beside still waters / He restores my soul," she begins, gathering the momentum of gratitude as she moves on, and changing the *He* to *You*. "You prepare a table before me in the presence of my enemies / You anoint my head with oil, my cup overflows. / Surely goodness and mercy shall follow me all the days of my life / And I shall dwell in Your house my whole life long."

Nita, 67, also sets apart awakening as a natural time for thanksgiving. "Upon waking up, I do deep breathing. That's a simple thing, but as I age the simple things I didn't appreciate during the running years have become precious." The other end of the day, as we give ourselves over to sleep, is also a natural time to express gratitude toward the Mystery at the heart of the universe. When such practices become sacred components of our lives, we understand the truth of Wendell Berry's comment that "to live, we must daily break the body and shed the blood of Creation. When we do this knowingly, lovingly, skillfully, reverently, it is a sacrament. When we do it ignorantly, greedily, clumsily, destructively, it is a desecration."

When anthropologists began their first studies of tribal gift exchanges, they found these peoples knew how to avoid such desecration. They didn't store up gifts or add them to their holdings in the form of wealth; instead, they passed them on. When they received gifts of food, they consumed them, but then substituted another food gift, sending it to the next community of receivers.

Throughout the world, enjoyment of the gift of food provides the most universal time for thanksgiving. Although no gift is more ordinary, none is more essential. Religious traditions acknowledge this in such practices as saying grace before and after meals. More extended liturgies include the Passover Seder that is one long expression of thanksgiving; the ceremonial potlatch of the northwestern North American tribes; and the Christian Eucharist, a Greek word that means "thanksgiving" not only for bread and wine, but for all the Holy One's gifts—from creation and incarnation to the death and resurrection of the Christ.

Today, women influenced by feminist and womanist movements regularly create rituals rooted in such practices. Typically, in women's gatherings, the gift of leadership itself is shared around a circle, rather than imposed from the top down, and the role of chairperson—if there is such a role—rotates.

Several years ago, the Sisters of Mercy of the United States enacted a circling of gifts dubbed by their founder, Catherine McAuley, as a "Grand Right and Left," a dance form where partnering is exchanged with everyone in the group, as in a reel or square dance. The Sisters engaged every one of the Mercy Motherhouses—from Belmont, North Carolina, to Pittsburgh, Pennsylvania, to Burlingame, California—in a creative potlatch where gifts of sculpture, painting, quilting, or some other art form were sent from one group to the next. As each community offered hospitality to these artworks, they carefully removed one of them and then replaced it with one of their own.

Lilly Rivlin, a Jubilarian who is an independent filmmaker, captures a similar circular process in a video called "Miriam's Daughters Now." One of the rituals she films is a women's Passover Seder—like all Seders, a meal of thanksgiving. Rivlin begins by panning tables where food is laid out to stress that the ceremony actually begins in the kitchen with the preparation and cooking of the meal.

Sitting in a circle, the women express gratitude. They give thanks for the Miriams who bore them, led them out of slavery, took them across the Red Sea, and danced with them when they got to the other side. They express gratitude to the first Miriam who actually did these things and not only—as in more traditional Seders—to her brothers Moses and Aaron. Thanksgiving moves from participant to participant, as women celebrate still other Miriams: foremothers who worked for tenants' rights on the lower East Side of New

York, women who've cared for their children, elders who've mentored them, and parents who've ennobled them. The Seder concludes with a rousing *"Dayenu,"* the traditional Jewish thanksgiving prayer (the phrase, pronounced *die-AY-noo,* means "it would have been enough"). In this version, each woman singles out a divine gift—as we do in Exercise 4—using the ritual affirmation *"dayenu."* Some give thanks in

---

EXERCISE 4

Dayenu: It Would Have Been Enough

At the Passover Seder, gratitude is expressed for deliverance and liberation from slavery, for guidance in crossing the sea, for Shabbat, for Torah. In this exercise, we similarly give thanks for our own people's histories. Then we move to gifts unique to us as individuals. We conclude with expressions of gratitude for food. Ideally, this is an exercise practiced in a group.

1. Begin by centering and attending to your breath, using the word *dayenu* as a centering word for a period of three to five minutes.
2. Think of a deliverance or liberation that is part of your ethnic, racial, or national history. Then, around the circle, give thanks for this liberation, using the phrase, "If You had freed my people, who are _____ [Leb-

the form of a wish: "If women had written the Haggadah, and placed mothers where they belong in history, *dayenu*" or "If our mothers had been honored for their daughters as well as their sons, *dayenu*." Others pray in acknowledgment: "If You had been with us only in our liberation from slavery, or in our crossing of the sea, or in the gift of Shabbat, *dayenu*."

anese, Korean, Mexican, etc.], only from _____, it would have been enough. *Dayenu*."

3. Now think of a deliverance or liberation that is part of your personal history. Around the circle, give thanks for this liberation, using the phrase, "If You had freed me only from _____, it would have been enough. *Dayenu*."

4. Now think of a way that food has been a liberation and/or of a particular meal for which you are grateful. (Or conversely, think of a way you've been enslaved by and then freed from abuse of food.) Around the circle, give thanks for food, using the phrase, "If You had given only the food [or the meal] of _____, it would have been enough. *Dayenu*."

In each case, after five women have spoken, the entire group sings the refrain, "*Dayenu*." If you aren't Jewish and don't know it or no Jewish women are in the group, ask one of your Jewish friends to teach it to you.

GRATITUDE AND EVIL

"My twin died at 50 last year, from cancer," writes Jan. "I'm still mourning her."

"My son is 32; AIDS takes a part of him away from me every day," Audrey reveals.

"My father was killed in a head-on collision between a truck and the car we were in," 63-year-old Joan says quietly, "and my brain was so badly damaged I've had to leave my job and learn to live with recurring seizures."

Tragedy—personal and global—is with us always. Homelessness and unemployment are epidemic. Violence frightens all citizens, especially older women, threatening to lock us inside our homes. Not only Sarajevo and Beirut, but many U.S. urban centers are in ruins. Our world is full of evil: cancer and AIDS and brain seizures. Vehicular homicide and bombed cities and teenagers with assault weapons. Families without shelter and men and women without work. Hunger precluding the saying of any grace.

How, in such a world, can we speak of gratitude?

I remember the first person who asked me that question. We were in a classroom, and the course was called "Education for Justice." I was teaching about thanksgiving and, as I did, noticed one of the students becoming more and more visibly angry until finally she erupted. "How, in a world filled with hatred and evil," she challenged me, "*how* can you speak of gratitude?"

Ironically, the mystery of evil and the mystery of gratitude are inextricably connected. Our refusal to tolerate evil comes as a direct result of realizing that the gifts of life belong to everyone. When we confront disease, violence, genocide, or any of the terrible wrongs in our world, we do so because we've got a spiritual conviction. When we volunteer in an AIDS hospice or serve in a soup kitchen, we do so based on a strong, intuitive belief. Health, peace, food, shelter, and employment are universal gifts. There's a fault line in the universe, however, that prevents those gifts from reaching all but a privileged minority of the world's people. Some call the fault line evil; theologians call it sin.

But theologians also teach that where sin abounds, grace abounds even more. Goodness already exists in our world—to believe otherwise is to give in to despair—but it's partial goodness, incomplete goodness. The fitting human response to evil and the way in which we can fulfill our potential for goodness is to accept our responsibility to all of the earth's creatures and try to repair the inequality, deprivation, and brokenness that prevent things from being as they ought.

But before we take action, we must pause to give thanks for the ordinary and pervasive gifts of life. Gratitude is not only the final ritual, it's the initial one too. Paradoxically, the starting point in facing evil is not the prophetic stand against it. The starting point is the genuflection of thanksgiving.

This is precisely where gratitude kindles artistic imagination. The disposition to be grateful awakens the realization that the Giver's gifts haven't yet reached everyone, thereby illuminating our interdependence with all creatures. It impels us to create forms and rituals to liberate others, just as the rituals of Jubilee Time have liberated us. It forces us onto our knees in prayer and back onto our feet in protest against injustice. The poetic insight of Nobel laureate Pär Lagerkvist gives expression to this dynamic:

May my heart's disquiet never vanish
May I never be at peace;
May I never be reconciled to life nor to death either;
May my path be unending.

It's a strange prayer. Yet if we pray it attentively, we realize the prayer for disquiet, in the face of gifts denied, is a petition we pray when we're quiet. When we allow ourselves to "be peace"—the phrase is Thich Nhat Hanh's—we hear the pain of those whose peace has been vandalized. When we are most reconciled within ourselves and with others, we are also reconciled to our unending call to stand against the power of evil.

GRATITUDE AND DYING

In the concluding passage of *Pilgrim at Tinker Creek,* Annie Dillard muses, "I think that the dying pray at the last not 'please,' but 'thank you,' in the same way guests thank their hosts at the door. Falling from airplanes the people are crying thank you, thank you, all down the air." As Jubilee Time moves toward its close, we partner the no of living against evil with the rueful and accepting yes of living toward dying. That yes inevitably includes gratitude addressed to a sacred Presence whom we thank at the exit door of our lives.

Each woman says her yes and her thank-you in her own unique way. Seventy-one-year-old Helen's summation of it is, "I think a lot about death and what awaits me when that time comes. Sometimes I say, 'It would be great to have the energy of youth with the wisdom which has come in the past twenty years.' However, I choose the latter." Phoebe, 63, says her yes with hope. "Age is the best time of my life and I'm optimistic that with good eating habits and exercise I will be in good shape until I die." And 68-year-old Mary Jean says it with humor. "OK. I do have this philosophy that 'Growing old is a matter of mind. If you don't mind, it doesn't matter.' But I've had great models in both my mom and dad and I hope to retain my senses and my wit up to my dying breath."

Our perspective on dying will almost certainly include ambivalence, the "thoughts about death and some unease about it" that 72-year-old Denise admits. Seventy-year-old Rosemary writes, "I have mixed feelings at this time in my life. I have fears of being long in the deterioration and dying process. Yet I'm grateful for the care and concern of those around me; grateful that I'm not expected to do and be what I can no longer do and be."

The acceptance of death as a constant companion is characteristic of Jubilee women. Although in our forties and fifties we might have tried to evade or ignore its inevitability, the majority of women I interviewed view dying as part of life's tapestry. Although they realize the far country of death itself can't be described, they acknowledge dying as a necessary part of living, setting it in the larger pattern of gratitude for life. In this, they are like Florida Scott-Maxwell, whom we met in the Threshold ritual. Well into her eighties, she acknowledges the pain of losing life, but interprets that pain philosophically: "The pain of losing good is the measure of its goodness. You need only claim the events of your life to make yourself yours. When you truly possess all you have been and done, which may take some time, you are fierce with reality. When at last age has assembled you together, will it not be easy to let it all go, lived, balanced, over?"

EXERCISE 5

Celebrating Our Life at the Time of Our Death

This exercise is an opportunity to create a memorial service celebrating our life in preparation for the time of our death. The ritual follows the framework of Jubilee Time, moving from Threshold to Gratitude and drawing on the store of self-understanding we have gained in the previous rituals. The following questions and directions are an opportunity to shape this celebration, which is particularly valuable for a Jubilee group. Ideally, seven specific sessions should be given to this exercise.

Create seven folders, one for each ritual, in which you note your responses to the following questions. Give copies of your wishes to those who are closest to you, to be used in a memorial service at the time of your death.

1. Which of your thresholds do you wish remembered? Make careful notes describing this for others. Choose music and a poem or other reading to accompany these memories. Name a person who will tell of your threshold-crossing during the service.
2. What kind of hallowing was evident in your life? How did you practice Sabbath? How did you let the land lie fallow? Choose music and a poem or other reading to

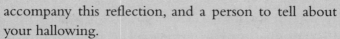

accompany this reflection, and a person to tell about your hallowing.

3. Which of your freedoms do you wish to memorialize? Make careful notes. Choose music and a poem or other reading to accompany them. Choose a person who will remember your exercise of freedom when the time comes for your service.

4. What do you believe has been your most significant journey? Where and to whom have you journeyed? What have you claimed on this journey; what have you given back? Make careful notes. Choose music and a poem or other reading to accompany your reflection. Choose someone to recount your journeys.

5. What do you wish remembered in the inventory of your possessions, powers, and relationships? How would you describe the work of your life? Choose music and a poem or other reading to accompany your notes. Choose someone to speak of your gathered inventory.

6. To whom and to what does your life story bear witness? In what way is it a gift or a model for other older women, helping to make their lives a Jubilee? Make careful notes in responding. Choose music and a poem or other reading to accompany them. Choose someone who will speak about your story.

7. To whom and to what do you wish to give thanks? For whom and for what? Make careful notes; choose one final piece of music, and a poem or other reading. Choose, finally, someone to speak your gratitude.

For centuries and generations, people on our planet have tended to say amen to this necessary letting go, even if unable to say what follows, even if resistant. Some assume the next stage is total silence; some nirvana; others reincarnation, resurrection of the body, or immortality of the soul. Many, like 58-year-old Connie, draw on some hope of afterlife. "I'm feeling less afraid of death," she says, about to start her sixtieth year, "and I feel strength in knowing there is another 'life' to experience after this." Others, like Ida Rollins, dying from cancer, choose the moment of their deaths, as she did, assisted by her daughter Betty. Others, like Edna St. Vincent Millay, admit death's finality, writing, "So it is, and so it will be, for so it has been, time out of mind." Yet, like her, they resist. "I know. But I do not approve. And I am not resigned."

Still others deliberately prepare for dying by designing their own memorial services. (See Exercise 5.)

GRATITUDE AND BEING

We begin Jubilee Time as we begin life: in wonder. The thresholds of later life intrigue us, and make us sensitive to the new worlds they introduce. Sabbath and hallowing deepen our awareness of these worlds as we claim our freedom and then make the healing journeys of life's second half. After those journeys, we complete our inventories and fashion our unique stories, and the energy of these rituals propels us into their summation, gratitude. Gratitude then returns us to wonder. With the clarity that only the fullness of years can bring, we marvel now that so much has been given. That our bodies, faithful companions, continue to work, even if with difficulty.

That even when our bodies lose the battle with disease, or our minds begin to fail us, we can choose either waiting or letting go. But perhaps most of all, we marvel that we have reached the culminating, defining moment when Being replaces Having and Doing.

The movement from Having—a house, a piece of land, a husband, a lover, a profession—to Being recurs constantly in spiritual lore on aging. The Taoist philosopher Chuang Chou says that *wu-wei,* nonaction, provides the key to our being—recalling for Jubilee women the not-doing of Sabbath and the years spent learning to let the land lie fallow. The *Tao Te Ching* agrees, teaching that in the end, the "doer will fail" and the "holder will lose." Jubilee Time has fostered such discoveries, helping us give up possessions in the mature realization we are not what we have, but what we are.

Drawing on Jewish roots, Rabbi Abraham Joshua Heschel offers similar wisdom, teaching that only three things are necessary to spirituality as we grow older: God, a soul, and a moment. If we cherish these three, we can attain what the rabbi calls "significant being." When we do, our mantra becomes an expression of simplest wisdom: "Just to be is a blessing; just to live is holy."

Arriving at this conviction is never easy, even as living and dying aren't easy. Being is not equivalent to withdrawal from life. Instead, Being concentrates life in a powerful center point, as a magnifying glass concentrates sunlight on paper, igniting the paper into flame. Being is the state of grace entered by wise old women who have forgone frenzied activity and busyness. These are the Jubilee women content to sit weaving in the sun or embroidering at the table of life with a readiness for whatever necessary work calls them. These older women are us.

Over the last several years, I have been a privileged witness to Jubilee women's testimony to the power of such being. "I am more free to speak about issues because my answers come from my 'core,' my inner center, seasoned with life experiences," writes 57-year-old Mary Jo. She chooses the biblical image of the deer that longs for running streams as her image for herself in life's second half. "I like to think of myself as being as full of energy and vitality as the deer that frolic on the fields outside my window. On the other hand, I also long to spend quiet time by the silent streams, wanting to rest and just 'Be.' "

Fifty-year-old Noel, a midwestern writer, describes a similar disposition toward Being. Having come back from what she calls "a profoundly devastating place carrying gifts from that dark journey across a new threshold to Life," she cites her critical dependence on the contemplative center within her. "Silence, solitude, meditation and early morning sitting in prayer each day are essential to my spiritual well-being and, I find, to my physical and psychological states too. I see much bigger pictures even as I'm content with the process called Life."

Concluding this ritual, we recognize that we too are privileged witnesses to the testimonies of Jubilee women: testimonies like Mary Jo's, coming from our inner cores and seasoned by our lives' experiences; testimonies like Noel's, nourished by silence, solitude, and prayer. We too carry gifts from dark and difficult journeys; we too see bigger pictures as we embrace the process called life.

The privileged experience of such witness comes from membership in the community of women who inhabit life's second half—a community some of us entered thirty or forty years ago, some of us only recently. But the privileged experience comes from the witness of our own lives too. As each ritual has unveiled another facet of Jubilee spirituality, and as Gratitude has made clear, a basic, fundamental truth underlies Jubilee Time: our existence is a jubilee, holy to us, holy throughout the generations, holy across the firmament. The praise and honor and jubilation we have directed toward the Giver now return full circle to reside, finally, in us. As they do, we feel an anointing that releases us to be Jubilee to the world.

In the human story, as we have aged into wisdom, women elders have suspected—and when we've been liberated from servitude, realized—this is why we are on earth. In our own century, we have finally gained access to the systems and the structures, the institutions and the freedoms that authorize and license us to express it. Though we may not have used the language of Jubilee, we have known that within ourselves we possess the power of the explorer to cross any threshold that confronts us, the power of the contemplative to sit still and wait upon the artistic moment, the power of the liberator to dispense with chains. We have known we possess the power of the pilgrim to journey back and down to ancestral places, the power of the householder to assess life's portions, the power of the storyteller to give voice to memory.

In this ritual we have bared the power of the Giver and the gift. Honoring these, and trying to do justice to them and to all that has preceded them, we take Jubilee Time's final step. We gather each of our powers, with the loveliness and the longing, the loss and the mourning, the music and the dancing that have accompanied them. And then, prayerfully, and joined in imagination with all of the world's women elders past, present, and future, we give our powers to the world. Fierce with reality and supported by one another, we pour our gifts into the earth's cup. We pour and pour until the cup is full and overflowing and the earth is drenched with our offerings. And then we let go, savoring the meaning of our lives as Jubilee and willing to renew the offering as often as we must until the trumpets sound everywhere, the prisoners are released, and age and celebration embrace.

$\mathcal{A}$PPENDIX

1. What have you discovered is the best thing—or things—about growing older?

2. What's the worst thing (if there is any)?

3. Do you have an image or a picture or a song or book title you would use to describe this time of life? Why this image or picture or title?

4. Would you briefly respond to the question, "How do you *feel* about growing older?"

5. What is something (some things) you know now that you didn't when you were younger? Something life has taught you?

6. Are there any practices or exercises (physical and/or spiritual), including community and/or political action, that assist you as you grow older?

7. Any additional comments?

Name:
Address:
Age: (If you prefer, put decade, e.g., 60s, 70s, etc.)
Race and/or ethnic origin:
Work involvement, past or present:
Country you live in:
Check one: In answering this questionnaire, I agree to have
            my comments used in Maria's book
            (Bantam, due 1995)
            (a) _____ without my name being used;
            (b) _____ if a fictitious name is used;
            (c) _____ using my own name;
            (d) _____ my comments are not for publication.
Thank you. Please return to: Maria Harris
                             P.O. Box 1405
                             Montauk, New York 11954

$\mathcal{N}$OTES

INTRODUCTION

p. xx. Margaret Mary Funk, "The Sabbath, or Don't We Have Time?" in *P.A.C.E.* (Winona, MN: St. Mary's Press, 1980).

p. xx. Abraham Joshua Heschel, *The Earth Is the Lord's* and *The Sabbath* (New York: Harper and Row, 1966).

p. xxi. Maria Harris, *Women and Teaching* (Mahwah, NJ: Paulist Press, 1988); *Dance of the Spirit: The Seven Steps of Women's Spirituality* (New York: Bantam, 1989).

p. xxiii. Sharon H. Ringe, *Jesus, Liberation, and the Biblical Jubilee* (Philadelphia: Fortress, 1985).

p. xxiii. John Howard Yoder, "The Implications of the Jubilee," in *The Politics of Jesus* (Grand Rapids: Eerdmans, 1972).

ONE: CROSSING THE THRESHOLD

p. 3. In "The Tree of Light Springs from the Threshold," Jo Milgrom speaks of the poetry of the threshold, using the words "threshold awe." In Doug Adams and Diane Apostolos-Cappadona, eds., *Art as Religious Studies* (New York: Crossroad, 1987), pp. 58–69.

p. 3. The Janus and Palestine comments are in G. van der Leeuw, *Re-*

ligion in Essence and Manifestation (London: George Allen and Unwin, 1933), p. 396.

p. 5. Orientation as a key element of the threshold is found in Bernard Goldman, *The Sacred Portal* (Detroit: Wayne State University Press, 1966), p. 21.

p. 6. In this book, women's personal comments are used with permission and the great majority come from the questionnaires I noted in the Introduction. Most women preferred using their own names, but I have changed the names of those who didn't. Ages are as reported. Where comments come from published or unpublished written work or were part of a public lecture, the notes reflect this.

p. 7. On rites of passage, see Mircea Eliade, *The Sacred and the Profane* (New York: Harcourt Brace Jovanovich, 1959), pp. 180–88.

p. 7. On ageism, see Robert Butler's description of his introduction of this term in *Why Survive? Being Old in America* (New York: Harper and Row, 1975), esp. pp. 11–16.

p. 10. Irene Fine, *The Wise Woman: A Celebration* (San Diego: Women's Institute for Continuing Jewish Education, 1988). She cites Savina Teubel, who planted the tree with the words reported (pp. 30–31); Audrey Karsh, who describes the ritual of wearing a special brooch that belonged to her paternal grandmother (p. 26); and Marleen Brasefield as the donor of the S.O.W. awards (p. 27). Her own comments on tearing up, giving away, burning, and removing are on page 17.

p. 13. Florida Scott-Maxwell, *The Measure of My Days* (New York: Knopf, 1978), pp. 13–14.

p. 14. Martha Whitmore Hickman reports fictionally on some of these thresholds in *Fullness of Time: Short Stories of Women and Aging* (Nashville: Upper Room Books, 1990).

p. 14. Elaine Cumming and William Henry, *Growing Old: The Process of Disengagement* (New York: Basic Books, 1961), p. 211.

p. 18. Judy Small sings of various understandings of bereavement in "No Tears for the Widow," *Snapshot* (Sandstock Music: New South Wales, 1990).

p. 20. May Sarton, *At Seventy* (New York: Norton, 1984), p. 147.

p. 28. From the obituary notice of Dame Judith Anderson in *The New York Times*, January 4, 1992, p. 9.

TWO: THE HALLOWING OF SABBATH

p. 29. John Peatling formulated this response as "I know I can do it but I don't want to." See his "Liturgical Suggestions for Celebrating the Para-Feasts of the Lord of All Distributions, the Holy Probability, Blessed Student and the Memory of Kurt Godel," in Gloria Durka and Joanmarie Smith (eds.), *Aesthetic Dimensions of Religious Education* (New York: Paulist Press, 1979), p. 132.

p. 35. On Sabbath, see Abraham Joshua Heschel, *The Sabbath*.

p. 36. The friend was Roger Hazelton, who recounts the exchange in his *Ascending Flame, Descending Dove* (Philadelphia: Westminster, 1975), pp. 64–65.

p. 41. See Elizabeth Johnson, *Women, Earth, and Creator Spirit* (New Jersey: Paulist, 1993), p. 34. Johnson is a scholar and theologian who won the 1993 Grawemeyer Award, awarded by the University of Louisville for outstanding religious book. See her *She Who Is: The Mystery of God in Feminist Theological Discourse* (New York: Crossroad, 1993).

p. 42. See Rene Dubos, *A God Within* (New York: Charles Scribner's Sons, 1972) for a classic statement on Franciscan and Benedictine spiritualities as they relate to the earth.

p. 49. Martin Buber, *Between Man and Man* (London: Routledge and Kegan Paul, 1946), pp. 8–11.

p. 51. Baba Copper, *Over the Hill: Reflections on Ageism Between Women* (Freedom, CA: Crossing, 1988), p. 75.

p. 51. Evelyn Eaton Whitehead, "Religious Images of Aging: An Examination of Themes in Contemporary Christian Thought," in Carol LeFevre and Perry LeFevre (eds.), *Aging and the Human Spirit: A Reader in Religion and Gerontology* (Chicago: Exploration, 1985), pp. 56–57.

p. 52. In *Listening: Journal of Religion and Culture* 12, 2 (Spring 1977), James Whitehead points out that the themes of uselessness and emptiness are examples of the ancient spiritual path of the *Via Negativa,* which lets pain be pain, and accepts uselessness and emptiness as components in all life (p. 80).

p. 53. The Care myth comes from Martin Heidegger's *Being and Time.* Translated by John Macquarrie and Edward Robinson (New York: Harper and Row, 1962), p. 242.

p. 53. On the power of one adult caregiver, see Gloria Steinem, *Revolution from Within* (Boston: Little, Brown, 1992), pp. 82ff.

THREE: PROCLAIMING FREEDOM

p. 57. Jenny Joseph, "Warning," from *Selected Poems* (Newcastle-upon-Tyne: Bloodaxe Books, 1992).

p. 59. On amnesty as biblical root of Jubilee, see Ringe, *Jesus, Liberation and the Biblical Jubilee,* pp. 22ff.

p. 63. See U.S. State Department report in *The New York Times* (February 3, 1994).

p. 67. In Gail Sheehy, "The Flaming Fifties," *Vanity Fair* (October 1993), p. 272.

p. 68. For an extended development of this theme, see Betty Friedan, *The Fountain of Age* (New York: Simon and Schuster, 1993).

p. 70. This is a point Gail Sheehy makes in *The Silent Passage* (New York: Random House, 1992), pp. 45–46.

p. 72. *Bhagavad Gita,* translated by Swami Prabhavananda and Christopher Sherwood (New York: Mentor Books, 1956).

p. 73. Gabriel Moran, *Religious Education Development: Images for the Future* (Minneapolis: Winston, 1983), p. 155.

p. 75. For this section on Jubilee, I am particularly indebted to John Howard Yoder, *The Politics of Jesus.*

p. 75. Most scripture texts are from NRSV. In some cases, I have changed them slightly to make them more gender sensitive.

p. 76. For this historical note on prisoners, see Gretchen Pritchard, "Living by the Word: Good News," *Christian Century* (December 1, 1993), p. 1203.

p. 76. Jean Harris, *They Always Call Us Ladies: Stories from Prison* (New York: Charles Scribner's Sons, 1988), pp. 64–65.

p. 80. Muriel Rukeyser, "Kathe Kollwitz," III, stanza 4. In *The Speed of Darkness* (New York: Random House, 1968), p. 103.

p. 81. See *Shortchanging Girls, Shortchanging America* (Washington: AAUW, 1991); *How Schools Shortchange Girls* (Washington: AAUW, 1992); *A Capella: A Report on the Realities, Concerns, Expectations and Bar-*

riers Experienced by Adolescent Women in Canada (Ottawa: Canadian Teachers Federation, 1990); Lyn Mikel Brown, *Meeting at the Crossroads* (Cambridge: Harvard University Press, 1992); Judith A. Dorney, *Courage to Act in a Small Way* (Cambridge: Harvard University Graduate School of Education, 1992), unpublished dissertation.

p. 81. Kate Douglas Wiggin, *Rebecca of Sunnybrook Farm* (New York: Grosset and Dunlap, 1903), p. 27.

p. 81. Reported in Lyn Mikel Brown and Carol Gilligan, "The Psychology of Women and the Development of Girls," unpublished paper presented at a conference held at the Cleveland Clinic Center Hotel, April 5, 1990, p. 18.

p. 84. In Marilyn Sewell, ed., *Cries of the Spirit* (Boston: Beacon, 1991), pp. 252–53.

p. 86. Ntozake Shange, *For Colored Girls Who Have Considered Suicide When the Rainbow Is Enuf* (New York: Macmillan, 1977), p. 63.

FOUR: THE JUBILEE JOURNEYS

p. 88. See Diedrick Snoek, "A Male Feminist in a Women's College Classroom," in Margo Culley and Catherine Portuges, eds., *Gendered Subjects: The Dynamics of Feminist Teaching* (Boston: Routledge and Kegan Paul, 1985), p. 138.

p. 94. Catherine Hanf Noren, *The Camera of My Family* (New York: Knopf, 1976). A videotape with the same title and including many of these pictures is available from the Jewish Anti-Defamation League.

p. 96. See, for example, Elizabeth Debold, Marie Wilson, and Idelisse Malave, *Mother Daughter Revolution* (Reading, MA: Addison-Wesley, 1993).

p. 98. Audre Lorde, *Sister Outsider* (Freedom, CA: Crossing, 1984), p. 42.

p. 99. Martha Robbins, *Midlife Women and Death of Mother: A Study of Psychohistorical and Spiritual Transformation* (New York: Peter Lang, 1990).

p. 100. In Marion Woodman, *Leaving My Father's House: A Journey to Conscious Femininity*. With Kate Danson, Mary Hamilton, and Rita Greer Allen. (Boston: Shambhala, 1992), pp. 225–27.

p. 102. Robbins, *Midlife Women,* p. 153.

p. 102. *Ibid.,* p. 197.

p. 105. One such forgiveness counselor is Robin Casarjian. See her *Forgiveness: A Bold Choice for a Peaceful Heart* (New York: Bantam, 1992), pp. 88–89, from which exercise 5 is adapted.

p. 108. On Medusa, see Catherine Keller, *From a Broken Web: Separation, Sexism and Self* (Boston: Beacon, 1986), pp. 50–56; pp. 67ff.

p. 111. For the Inanna-Erishkegal story, I have drawn on Belle Debrida, "Drawing from Mythology in Women's Quest for Selfhood," in Charlene Spretnak, ed., *The Politics of Women's Spirituality* (Garden City: Doubleday, 1982), pp. 138–51; from Sylvia Brinton Perera, *Descent to the Goddess: A Way of Initiation for Women* (Toronto: Inner City Books, 1981), to which Jean Thompson introduced me; and from Judith Ochshorn, "Ishtar and her Cult," in Carl Olson, ed., *The Book of the Goddess Past and Present* (New York: Crossroad, 1988), pp. 16–28. The chant is found in James B. Pritchard, *Ancient Near Eastern Texts Relating to the Old Testament* (Princeton: Princeton University Press, 1955), p. 53.

p. 113. In *The Crone: Woman of Age, Wisdom and Power* (San Francisco: Harper and Row, 1985), Barbara G. Walker relates the belief that with menopause, although the menstrual blood no longer flowed outside the body, it was retained. Known as "wise blood," it was regarded as the source of old women's wisdom (p. 49).

FIVE: TAKING INVENTORY

p. 117. Hickman tells a lovely story of a garage sale in "The Last Hour," in *Fullness of Time.* op. cit.

p. 118. Virginia Woolf, *Three Guineas* (New York: Harcourt Brace Jovanovich, 1966), pp. 80ff. First published 1938.

p. 118. Virginia Woolf, *A Room of One's Own* (New York: Harcourt Brace Jovanovich, 1957). First published 1929.

p. 121. Source is the Older Women's League, Greater New York Chapter. See also Ginita Wall and the editors of Consumer Reports Books' work entitled *Our Money, Ourselves* (Yonkers, NY: Consumer Reports Books, 1992).

p. 128. Sarton, *At Seventy,* p. 172.

p. 129. See Elizabeth Janeway, *Powers of the Weak* (New York: Knopf, 1980), especially chapters 11 and 12.

p. 129. Quoted in Joan Chittister, *Job's Daughters: Women and Power* (Mahwah, NJ: Paulist, 1990), p. 9.

p. 129. Jurgen Habermas, "Hannah Arendt: On the Concept of Power," in *Philosophical and Political Profiles,* translated by Frederick Lawrence (Cambridge: M.I.T. Press, 1983), pp. 310ff. Cited in Chittister, *Job's Daughters.*

p. 131. This is recounted in Madonna Kolbenschlag, "Spirituality: Finding Our True Home," in Madonna Kolbenschlag, ed., *Women in the Church I* (Washington, DC: Pastoral Press, 1987), p. 210.

p. 133. Quoted in Carolyn Heilbrun, *Writing a Woman's Life* (New York: Norton, 1988), p. 109.

p. 136. In Betty Friedan, *The Fountain of Age* (New York: Simon and Schuster, 1993), pp. 24–25.

SIX: TELLING OUR STORY

p. 143. See Judith Plaskow Goldenberg with Karen Bloomquist, Margaret Early, and Elizabeth Farians, "Epilogue: The Coming of Lilith," in Rosemary Radford Ruether (ed.), *Religion and Sexism* (New York: Simon and Schuster, 1974), pp. 341–43. For Plaskow's further and more recent comment on the story, see her *Standing Again on Sinai* (San Francisco: Harper and Row, 1990), pp. 54–55.

p. 144. Although the use of *story* as a verb is rare, it is acceptable English—see both the *OED* and the *American Heritage Dictionary of the English Language.* I use it to capture the active power in the word, and to signify it as a ritual act.

p. 146. Robert N. Butler, "The Life Review: An Interpretation of Reminiscence of the Aged," *Psychiatry* 26 (1963), pp. 65–76.

p. 147. Rose Dobrof, "Introduction," in Mark Kaminsky, ed., *The Uses of Reminiscence* (New York: Haworth, 1984), p. xviii.

p. 147. Robert Butler, *Why Survive? Being Old in America* (New York: Harper and Row, 1975).

p. 147. *Ibid.,* p. 413.

p. 147. Heilbrun, *Writing a Woman's Life,* p. 30.

p. 147. Scott-Maxwell, *The Measure of My Days;* May Sarton, *Journal of a Solitude* (New York: Norton, 1973); *At Seventy* (New York: Norton, 1984); *Encore: A Journal of the Eightieth Year* (New York: Norton, 1993).

p. 148. Doris Grumbach, *Coming Into the End Zone* (New York: Norton, 1991), pp. 48, 251.

p. 148. Sarah and A. Elizabeth Delany, *Having Our Say: The Delany Sisters' First 100 Years* with Amy Hill Hearth (New York: Kodansha International, 1993).

p. 149. *Encore* ceased publishing in mid-1995.

p. 150. Arisa Victor, "The Grandmother Archetype," *Encore* vol. 1, no. 6 (September/October, 1993); Faye Cameron, "At 87—Making Music With My Life," *Encore* vol. 1, no. 3 (March/April 1993), p. 22; Viola Q. Seligo, "At 90—Still Wondering," *ibid.,* p. 23.

p. 151. Natalie Goldberg, *Writing Down the Bones: Freeing the Writer Within* (Boston: Shambhala, 1986); Christina Baldwin, *Life's Companion: Journal Writing as a Spiritual Quest* (New York: Bantam, 1991); Gail Ranadive, *Writing Re-Creatively: A Spiritual Quest for Women* (Mt. Vernon, VA: Columbine, 1992).

p. 153. Peter Coleman, *Ageing and Reminiscence Processes* (New York: Wiley, 1986).

p. 154. Kathleen Woodward, *Aging and Its Discontents* (Bloomington: Indiana University Press, 1991). On the Life Review, see her "Reminiscence and the Life Review: Prospects and Retrospects," in Thomas R. Cole and Sally A. Gadow eds., *What Does It Mean to Grow Old?* (Durham, NC: Duke University Press, 1986), pp. 159–61. The research cited by Woodward that makes these points is found in Virginia Revere and Sheldon Tobin, "Myth and Reality: The Older Person's Relationship to His Past," *International Journal of Aging and Human Development* vol. 12, no. 1 (1980–81), pp. 15–26.

p. 154. Janet Bloom, "Minerva's Doll," in Kaminsky, *The Uses of Reminiscence,* pp. 116ff.

p. 158. "Three Stories Tall" was a family-oriented storytelling program hosted on a Washington, D.C., TV station several years ago by Jon

Spelman. See Anne Simpkinson, "Sacred Stories," *Common Boundary* (November/December 1993), p. 28.

p. 160. Allen B. Chinen has discovered and reinterpreted fifteen fairy tales directly concerned with elders in his *In the Ever After: Fairy Tales and the Second Half of Life* (Wilmette, IL: Chiron, 1989). See also Bruno Bettelheim, *The Uses of Enchantment* (New York: Knopf, 1976).

p. 168. For ways of using midrash with adults, see Jo Milgrom, *Handmade Midrash: Workshops in Visual Theology* (Philadelphia: The Jewish Publication Society, 1992). See also Plaskow, *Standing Again on Sinai,* pp. 53–57.

p. 172. Bruce Chatwin, *The Songlines* (New York: Viking, 1987).

SEVEN: THE SONG OF GRATITUDE

p. 174. Anne Morrow Lindbergh, *Gift from the Sea* (New York: Vintage, 1955), p. 43.

p. 179. See Thich Nhat Hanh, *Peace Is Every Step: The Path of Mindfulness in Everyday Life,* edited by Arthur Kotler (New York: Bantam, 1991), p. 23.

p. 184. Louis Dupre, "On Being a Christian Teacher of Humanities," *The Christian Century* (April 29, 1992), p. 455.

p. 186. Wendell Berry, *The Gift of Good Land* (San Francisco: North Point, 1981), p. 281.

p. 186. See Lewis Hyde, *The Gift* (New York: Random House, 1983).

p. 187. Lilly Rivlin, "Miriam's Daughters Now." Available from Lilly Rivlin, 463 West Street, Apt. 510A, New York, NY 10014. See Letty Cottin Pogrebin's extended description of years of such women's Seders in her *Deborah, Golda, and Me: Being Female and Jewish in America* (New York: Crown, 1991), pp. 111–27.

p. 191. See Gabriel Moran, "Religious Education for Justice," in *Interplay* (Winona, MN: St. Mary's Press, 1982), pp. 143–58.

p. 192. Pär Lagerkvist, *Evening Land/Aftonland,* translated by W. H. Auden and Leif Sjoberg (London: Souvenir, 1977), p. 141. Originally published 1953.

p. 192. See Thich Nhat Hanh, *Being Peace* (Berkeley: Parallax, 1987).

p. 192. Annie Dillard, *Pilgrim at Tinker Creek* (New York: Harper and Row, 1974), pp. 270–71.

p. 193. Scott-Maxwell, *The Measure of My Days,* p. 42.

p. 196. These are lines from Millay's "Dirge Without Music." In *The Mentor Book of Major American Poets,* edited by Oscar Williams and Edwin Honig (New York: New American Library, 1962), p. 419.

p. 197. Albert Chi-Lu Chung, "The Elderly and Moral Precepts in Chinese Tradition," in Francis V. Tiso, ed., *Aging: Spiritual Perspectives* (Lake Worth, FL: 1982), p. 58.

p. 197. *Ibid.*

p. 197. Quoted in Asher Finkel, "Aging: The Jewish Perspective," in Tiso, ed., *Aging,* p. 133.

p. 197. Erich Fromm elaborates on the distinction between having and being in *To Have or to Be* (New York: Bantam, 1981) (originally published 1976). See especially pp. 78–79.

$\mathcal{I}$NDEX

ABOUT THE AUTHOR

Maria Harris is a member of the Core Teaching Staff of Auburn Theological Seminary in New York, and Visiting Professor of Religious Education at New York University. She has been a member of the faculty of Fordham University and has held both the Howard Chair in Religious Education at Andover Newton Theological School in Massachusetts, and the Tuohy Chair in Interreligious Studies at John Carroll University in Cleveland. She has served as editor of the journal, *P.A.C.E.* (Professional Approaches for Christian Educators); book editor of the journal *Religious Education*; president of the Association of Professors and Researchers in Religious Education; and as an Associate Director of Religious Education in the Diocese of Rockville Centre, Long Island. Her publications include over seventy articles and twelve books.

Maria Harris has taught in universities, judicatories, and dioceses throughout the United States. These include Boston College, Fairfield, La Salle, Villanova, Regis, and Santa Clara Universities; Princeton, Union and Immaculate Conception Seminiaries; the Presbyterian School of Christian Education; Denver, Phoenix, Anchorage, Houston, St Petersburg, and San Francisco. She has lectured extensively beyond U.S. borders as well, in Korea, Bermuda, Australia, New Zealand, Germany, and the Netherlands. She has served as Scholar in Residence at Loyola University in Chicago, and delivered the Bradner Lectures at Episcopal Theological Seminary, the Madeleva Lecture at St. Mary's College, and the Schaff Lectures at Pittsburgh Theological Seminary, among others.

Maria divides her time between New York's Greenwich Village and Montauk, Long Island, where she lives with her husband, author and teacher Gabriel Moran.